Leap for Life®

*A Guide to Heart Disease Prevention
and Management*

This book is the personal property of:

LIBRARY OF CONGRESS CARD NUMBER 00-111859

ISBN 0-9706675-0-7

MANUFACTURED IN THE UNITED STATES OF AMERICA

Leap for Life®: A Guide to Heart Disease Prevention and Management

Printed and bound by Acorn Press, Lancaster, Pa.

Text design and composition by Sutter House, Lititz, Pa.

Cover design by Pat Ramseur

Medical illustrations by Jay McElroy

Additional copies of this book may be obtained by writing Leap for Life®, 411 North Washington, Suite 3100, Dallas, TX 75246 or by sending an e-mail to leap@baylordallas.edu.

Dedication

The Baylor Health Care System would like to dedicate this book to the following people:

Mr. and Mrs. William C. Pickens

Mary Alice and Mark Shepherd

Ernestine and Bradley Wayne

Each of these individuals has made substantial charitable donations to the Leap for Life® cardiovascular disease education program. Without their unprecedented generosity, Leap for Life® would not exist today. A heartfelt thank-you goes out to each of you.

About the Book

The authors have attempted to use a writing style that is easily understood; however, at times it was appropriate to use a medical term. For your convenience, there is a glossary of terms at the back of *Leap for Life®: A Guide to Heart Disease Prevention and Management.* The physicians referenced in this book or whose opinions or comments are expressed in the book are not employees or agents of Baylor Health Care System but are independent practicing physicians. *Leap for Life®: A Guide to Heart Disease Prevention and Management* provides easy to understand information on heart disease, much of which has been obtained from the knowledge of physicians, nurses, dietitians, social workers, exercise physiologists, pharmacists, and other health educators. The information in this book is not meant to take the place of the advice of your doctor. You should discuss any individual medical problems with your doctor. *Leap for Life®: A Guide to Heart Disease Prevention and Management* does not endorse any company or product. Leap for Life® is a trademark of the Baylor Health Care System.

SENIOR EDITOR
Kristine Lloyd Currie, M.S.

MEDICAL EDITOR
Cara East, M.D.

WRITERS

Jenny Adams, Ph.D.
Susan Adams, B.S.
Janet Bigej-Cerqua, B.S.N., R.N.
Lona Bryant, R.N.
Amy Castillo, M.S.
Teri Hernandez, B.S.N., R.N.
Robert Hutchison, Pharm.D.

Antonio Labellarte, Pharm.D.
Stacy Lofton, M.S., R.D., L.D.
Kay Penner, R.Ph.
Judy Rickard, L.M.S.W.
Jana Rupnow, B.S.
Jo Anne Spears, L.M.S.W., A.C.P.
Paul Yim, R.N.
Phyllis Yount, L.M.S.W., A.C.P.

Contents

Preface

The Leap for Life® program originated in 1995 at the Baylor Health Care System in Dallas, Texas. At the time, the purpose of Leap for Life® was to educate patients with heart disease who were unable to attend cardiac rehabilitation programs. The educational delivery method consisted of an all-day lecture that was usually held on Saturdays. Each participant received a three-ring binder including informational handouts that were covered in the class. A team from the hospital staff educated patients on topics including heart disease, medications, exercises, nutrition, and stress management. Shortly after the initial Leap for Life® workshop, the program was expanded to the Baylor Medical Centers at Dallas, Irving, Waxahachie, and Garland as well as the Baylor Hillside Senior Center.

Participants who attended a workshop took a pre- and post-test to evaluate program effectiveness. Individual participants also received telephone calls three, six, nine, and twelve months following the workshop to determine if they retained the information.

During the last five years, Leap for Life® has developed into a workshop for all patients with heart disease, not only those who are unable to attend cardiac rehabilitation programs. Rather than using a test for evaluation, the educators encourage participants to set personal goals and determine a plan for a healthy lifestyle. Within this new format, the participants receive telephone calls three, six, and twelve months following the workshop to determine progress on individual goals. In 1997, the three-ring binder was replaced with a 42-page book. This book has since been revised into the book you are now reading. All participants who attend a Leap for Life® workshop will receive a copy of this book.

In April 1999, the program was expanded once again to include Baylor Medical Center at Grapevine.

The mission and vision of Leap for Life® has always been the education, assistance, and risk factor modification of patients with cardiovascular disease or those at risk for the disease. Our team will continue this focus as we develop and progress in the new millennium.

—Kristine Lloyd Currie, M.S.
On behalf of the Baylor Health Care System
Leap for Life® team

Acknowledgements

The Baylor Health Care System would like to thank William "Bill" M. Day, Mary Ann McMullan, Marsha Rippy, and others who wish to remain anonymous for spending time recounting their successful personal battles with cardiovascular disease so that others may learn from their stories. We would also like to thank Michael Hooker, who has dedicated a significant amount of his personal time over the past four years to help make the community aware of the Leap for Life® program. Thank you, Mike, our Leap for Life® "star."

The Baylor Health Care System would also like to thank the following reviewers and contributors:

Ronald Aebersold, M.D.

Kristen Albani, M.S., R.D., L.D.

Pam Bortzfield, R.N.

Bill Currie, M.S., A.T.C., L.A.T.

Sandra K. Dunn, R.R.T.

Carey Elliot, R.N.

Karin Friday, B.S.N., R.N.

Allison Heinrich, R.D., L.D.

Karen Henry, R.D., L.D.

Sally Hill, R.N., C.D.E.

Sandy Knox, R.N., B.S.N., C.N.A.

Barbara McCloskey, Pharm.D., B.H.C.P.S., C.D.E.

Emily Malorzo, R.D., L.D.

Amy Myser, R.N.

Melissa Nelligan, M.B.A., C.F.R.E.

Terri Nuss, M.S.

Cynthia D. Orticio, M.A., E.L.S.

Sarah Pollex, M.P.H.

Trista Prasifka, R.D., L.D.

Michael (Mickey) Price, J.D.

Kevin Procious, B.S., M.C.P.

Wendy Segrest, M.S.

Dawn Shutter, M.S

Sue Simmons, R.R.T., R.C.P.

Jo Sullivan, J.D.

Remy Tolentino, M.S.N., R.N.

Robin Vogel

Stacey Waide, B.S., R.D., L.D.

Joe Weber, B.S.

Introduction

Leap for Life®: A Guide to Heart Disease Prevention and Management will help you understand your heart and vascular system and guide you on a journey to better health. It will give you information about various types of heart and vascular disease and tips on how to practice a healthy lifestyle. As your health should be a partnership between you and your doctor, this book is not meant to replace guidance from your doctors or other health care professionals. Share with your doctor the personal goals that you have set for yourself before beginning your plan. If you have specific questions about your disease, contact your doctor or health care provider.

As this book is meant to help answer questions you may have about heart disease, the chapters are presented in a question-and-answer format and there is a glossary in the back of the book.

Chapter 6 presents information about goal setting. After you write down your goals, you may want to post them on your office wall or somewhere you will see them daily, so you will remember to work towards them. Also, share your goals with family members or friends to help you accomplish what you have set out to do.

The following is a copy of an actual letter written by a heart patient and sent to his three sons.

February 2, 2000

Dear [Sons]—

I want to bring each of you up to date on my health and what I have been doing about it. I also want to share with you what I have learned and how it might affect each of you. Believe me, I am getting quite an education!

I first learned about a possible heart problem during a routine annual physical when my doctor did an electrocardiogram, which measures the performance of the heart in some electrical way. Since he did not like the results, he sent me to a heart specialist who proceeded to put me through a couple of tests to find out what was wrong, if anything. The first test was a stress test, which puts the heart under stress and then measures how it performs. Mine performed poorly. The next test involved putting me in the hospital and inserting a catheter into my groin and up into my heart, along with some dye in order to take a closer look. He found some blockage in two arteries and also diagnosed a weakened heart muscle.

I guess the bad news is that I have a problem or potential problem, but along with that the good news is that I can do a lot about this and possibly correct the situation and resume more perfect health.

I am now going to [a local] cardiac rehabilitation center to have a regular and increasingly more rigorous exercise program three days a week. I have to go for a total of 18 sessions, of which I have completed 10. During these exercises I am hooked up to radio-transmitted monitors and supervised by wonderful and professional cardiac nurses. I feel stronger each time and feel I am making real progress. Of course the final test will come after I complete the sessions and have another stress test performed by the cardiologist. I will let you know the result.

It was strongly suggested that I lose some weight, and I have managed to shed about twenty pounds so far with at least fifteen more to go. I also have to pay attention to my diet and eat a "heart-healthy" diet. I am still learning about that.

I also attend two educational sessions, where I learn all about the heart and cardiovascular problems. A big emphasis is learning about preventive things I can do to avoid future problems. I go again tomorrow and look forward to a lengthy lecture on diet. I then should be able to eat a lot smarter.

I want to share with you some of what I have learned because it may affect one or more of you, too. But first let me tell you a little about the group I exercise with and the people who are in the program, because to me this was a real surprise. We get to know each other at least a little and share information about ourselves and our health. I am one of the few people in the program who has not had open-heart surgery or perhaps a less invasive procedure. I am 63 and some are older than I and many are younger—a lot younger. I was impressed by this because it shows that heart disease and the problems it causes can happen at any age and to anyone. A couple of stories:

One man, about 60, is a marathon runner and has been for years. Last fall he planned to go to New York to run in the marathon but at the suggestion of his daughter, he had a physical exam. The doctor found he had a leaky heart valve, and he ended up in surgery having it repaired. The week before his diagnosis he told me he had run over 20 miles and had never broken a sweat. Who would have thought he had heart problems?

Another man is trim and apparently very athletic. About three months ago he had a heart attack and then a five-way heart bypass operation. He is only 38 years old!

I was sitting in the waiting room yesterday and overheard a conversation with two men in their thirties. Both had had complete heart transplant operations and were ready to begin cardiac rehabilitation. Imagine that for people only in their thirties!

I know I am in the program because I did not do what I knew I should have been doing all along. First, I let my weight get out of line and I ballooned up to about 200 pounds. That is a lot when you are only five-foot-seven. And I did not eat correctly, eating far too many fatty foods, especially ice cream. And last, I became too sedentary and did not exercise nearly enough. That has or is all changing.

In the education class last week, we delved into the causes of heart problems, and I share these with you now because one or more of them may affect each of you. These potential causes are called "risk factors" and they are divided into two groups.

The first group is called "uncontrollable risks."

Age—As we grow older the risk increases, and we all grow older. But what is older?

I have already cited examples of people in their thirties with problems, so just be aware that you too are getting older along with your old man. For men, after 45 years is the time to really pay attention.

Gender—The problem is more severe in men than in women.

Family history—This is the one to pay attention to because heart problems seem to follow in families, and yours is no exception. Just remember that my father died at age 56 of heart problems and his sister had heart disease, and I have a problem too so you have a family history of this on my side of the family. You also have it on your mother's side as both your grandmother and grandfather died of heart or cardiovascular disease. So it is extremely important that you recognize this family history and know that it comes down to each of you through both of your parents.

The second group is called the "controllable risks."

Smoking—This is the number one item and affects other diseases, too, such as cancer. Since as far as I know you are all non-smokers and very much against the practice, I won't dwell on it.

Cholesterol levels—This is a substance in the blood that is both good and bad. I won't go into detail, but if you are interested I will send you more information. When you get a blood test, the results should tell you about your cholesterol, and your doctor can interpret the results for you and tell you if you are in good shape or bad. But if it is out of line, it can be a killer.

Lack of exercise—I have learned that aerobic exercise is very important to the body, especially the heart muscle. When you get right down to it, [the heart] is really the most important muscle in the body and deserves a regular workout.

Overweight—Too much body fat puts extra work on the heart and causes all kinds of other problems. This is an important issue for me.

Blood pressure—Another issue for me because I have had high blood pressure for over 35 years and have been treated for it. I am now on new medication, and that is bringing it down to normal levels. But diet and exercise are important here too, as I am finding out. High blood pressure seems to run in the family on both sides, so you might want to keep an eye on yours. It should be less than 140/90.

Diabetes—Your doctor will check you for this and I have been warned that I could be pre-diabetic. [My doctor] thinks that diet and weight loss will eliminate this as an issue for me.

I hope you find all this as interesting as I do. I wanted to share this with you particularly in consideration of the history on both sides of the family. I hope none of you ever has a problem, but in the meantime I can only suggest that an annual physical checkup is well worth it, and if you have one, share the family history with your doctor. If any of the controllable risk factors is something you think you can do something about, that of course is up to you.

I have to take full responsibility for whatever genes and family history I pass along to each of you, and I wish I could apologize for that which is not so good. But I wanted to share all of this stuff with you so you can decide for yourselves what to do for follow-up. My motive in sending this is only that you each have a long and healthful life.

Much love as always,

Dad

Reprinted with permission, 2000.

I

Understanding Your Heart and Vascular System

Heart disease changes the lives of millions of people every day. It is the number one killer of men and women in the United States, yet many of us do not think about it until it happens to us or someone we care about. Then what? How do we deal with the physical and emotional changes that are often permanent?

Bill Day is a husband, a father, a grandfather, and a survivor. He was 63 years old and leading an active life in Dallas, Texas, when heart disease changed his approach to living. The following story is a true one, and much of it is in Bill's own words. Hopefully this story will help you understand what it might be like to live through a heart attack. Five months after his hospitalization for heart problems, Bill has to fight back tears to tell his story.

Bill had been a member of a local health club for quite some time. He had been having a burning sensation in his chest area during exercise for about seven months. He attributed this feeling to indigestion and was taking antacid medicine for it. He admits to taking as many as eight pills at a time to try to relieve the pain. Looking back, he says, "I think it was heart-related pain. I just did not recognize it."

In September 1999, Bill was sitting at work on a Monday morning when his right arm went numb. This was nothing new to him since he had noticed it five or six times before, so he just brushed it off as "no big deal." He did what he terms the "macho bit" and just tried to shake it off. But this day would be different than before. Ignoring the tingling sensation, he attempted to write something when the pen fell out of his hand. When he tried to pick it back up, his hand and fingers would not work properly and he could not grasp the pen. Still determined that nothing was wrong, he got up and went outside to talk with one of his employees, but he does not remember that conversation. He went back inside, sat down, and started feeling better. Shortly after that, he told his boss that he needed to go home. Within 20 minutes of his house he was feeling light-headed, so when he drove by a local hospital he decided to stop at the emergency department.

At the hospital, they got him right in and tried to determine what was happening. "They kept me on a monitor nearly all day. The doctor and nurses kept checking on me. They did not find anything right then. They set me up with all these tests with a doctor of internal medicine." After deciding he was not in immediate danger, the emergency department staff sent Bill home with an appointment to see a doctor who specializes in internal medicine. Bill says that he had a physical and blood test later that week and was then scheduled for an exercise stress test on the following Tuesday.

On Tuesday, Bill had the exercise stress test with an echocardiogram. This test allowed Bill's doctor to get a better picture of how well his heart was working. Bill was told that the treadmill would increase in speed and elevation every few minutes as he walked on it. At the end of the test he would lie on his side on the examination table. An instrument would be moved across his chest so that an image of his heart could be visualized on a monitor.

Four minutes into the stress test, Bill began to have difficulty breathing. He said he had an extreme pain in his chest and told the doctor that if the test were not stopped right then, he did not think he would make it. Bill describes the sensation he felt as a pressure in his chest and a dull pain. When asked for more details about the pain, he says, "Have you ever swallowed something and it goes down the wrong way and you can feel it all the way down? That is how it felt but much stronger and heavier. It felt like someone was standing on my chest."

At that point, the doctor told Bill that he was going to be admitted to the hospital right away. "That scared the fire out of me. By then I was already feeling better. Like I said, you go back to that macho thing, you know—I do not have heart attacks." The hospital staff took Bill directly to the coronary care unit so that he could be closely monitored. "I was scared and I called my wife and told her that they put me in the intensive care unit."

Bill had an angiogram that showed his cardiologist that Bill was going to need a procedure called an angioplasty, which would hopefully improve the blood flow to his heart. During an angioplasty, the doctor inserts a catheter into the arteries of the heart and blows up a small balloon to try and push the blockages out of the main flow of the artery. The angioplasty was scheduled for Thursday morning.

After the angioplasty, the cardiologist came in Bill's hospital room and told him that it had not worked. Two of Bill's arteries were completely blocked and a third one was 85% blocked. The cardiologist had already arranged for Bill to have heart surgery. Bill says, "When I came to, everything was already arranged." The surgery was scheduled for Monday morning.

"That wait was the longest three days of my life. They put me on a floor where everyone had heart problems, and there was another guy up there just like me; we were both getting surgery on Monday morning." Over that weekend the doctors came by to tell Bill what was going to happen on Monday. "I wanted all the information I could get," Bill says. Then, finally, Monday came.

The surgeons did five-vessel bypass surgery on Bill's heart that day. Bill says part of his heart was discolored, as was one artery. This discoloration results from the lack of blood supply to the artery and heart muscle. Fighting back tears, Bill says, "The surgeon told me that I was lucky."

Now Bill is able to joke a little about what happened to him and tells a story of the first time that a nurse helped him out of bed and into a chair. Bill said, "There is no way I am getting up out of this bed. You are crazy, man." The nurse reassured Bill that he could in fact do it, and proceeded to help Bill out of bed. When he did, blood drained from the bandages and got on the teddy bear that the hospital staff gave Bill after the surgery. Bill says, "I made them wash the teddy bear." He jokes that for a hospital bill as large as his was going to be, he thought the bear should be clean.

Bill says the worst experience he had with the surgery was waking up at night. Since his wife was not sleeping in the hospital with him, he was there at night alone with his thoughts. He says, "I was not hurting, but I was scared. You just wake up scared about what they have done. That is pretty huge."

Bill was finally released to go home six days after the surgery and says he was happy to be home but somewhat nervous about being on his own. His doctor recommended cardiac rehabilitation for Bill, so he enrolled in the local program. "When I first started rehabilitation I thought, no way. The nurse put me on the bicycle for five minutes and then the treadmill for five minutes. And she said go as fast or as slow as I thought I could. By the end, I used the whole hour for riding and walking."

He says that the staff members in rehabilitation watched him, and he built up a trust with them. Bill knew that the staff was teaching him to exercise at home just like in rehabilitation. Now at home, he walks for two miles and rides the bicycle six to seven miles (about twenty to thirty minutes). Bill says, "I do weights, but not stuff that stretches my chest. Cardiac rehabilitation was the best thing I ever did. I went for 12 weeks. I got the shirt and my picture made and everything. I would recommend that for everyone."

Bill and his family have changed their way of living since the surgery. Bill has lost 20 pounds and works out five times a week with his 13-year-old grandson. At Bill's last checkup with the doctor, his total cholesterol was down from 266 mg/dL to 165 mg/dL thanks to the help of a healthy lifestyle and medication. Bill says, "Between the rehabilitation and the diet things, we have changed our whole way of life. And that kind of makes it better, when you go to your doctor and you find out your cholesterol values. It has actually worked; it is working."

Bill says he hopes that in three to five years he will still be eating right and exercising. He jokes that he "joined the health club one year at a time. So if I don't go, my wife will be mad at me since I spent the money up front." Bill admits that a lifestyle change is going to take some work. He discloses, "I am sure it is not going to be easy. I have no doubt in my mind that I will eat prime rib before long—just like pizza. But you know, they tell you if you are going to eat pizza, just eat one piece. Well, why do I even want it if that is all I can have? There is no use in messing with it. That is my philosophy."

Although Bill says his chest area still bothers him a little, he has been able to put a positive spin on the whole situation and says through tears that he feels lucky. He admits he is still a little overweight, but he is still working on that and hopes he is "on the right track now." Bill smiles and says, "I feel better now than I have in two years."

This chapter will provide you with an overview of how your heart and vascular (blood vessels) system works. The "heart and vascular system" can also be called the "cardiovascular system." When you see the term "cardiovascular system" throughout the rest of this chapter, it will be used to describe the heart and vascular system.

By reading this chapter, you will learn about the heart and different types of cardiovascular disease. You will also learn about additional health problems that may occur and are related to or are a result of cardiovascular disease. Risk factors that can increase your chance of developing cardiovascular disease and additional health problems will be discussed next.

Part I

About My Heart

◆ What does my heart look like?

Your heart is a muscular organ that is hollow, has four chambers, and lies in the center of your chest, slightly to the left of your breastbone. Your heart is about the size of your fist and weighs less than one pound. There are three main arteries that lie on your heart and supply it with blood and oxygen: the circumflex artery, the left anterior descending artery, and the right coronary artery (Figures 1-1, 1-2). These arteries collectively are called the "coronary arteries."

FIGURE 1-1. Cross section of the heart with chambers

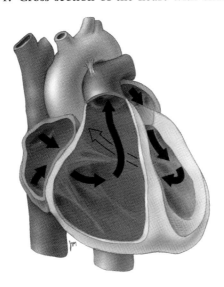

◆ How does my heart get its oxygen?

Oxygen is essential to all of the organs in your body, including your heart. Your body contains two different types of vessels, arteries and veins. An artery carries oxygen-rich blood to all parts of the body, and veins carry blood that is low in oxygen back to the heart and lungs (Figure 1-3). The coronary arteries, which lie on the outside of the heart and penetrate into the heart muscle, supply the heart muscle with oxygen-rich blood.

FIGURE 1-2. Outside of the heart showing coronary arteries

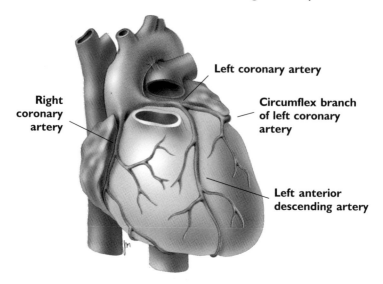

Right coronary artery

Left coronary artery

Circumflex branch of left coronary artery

Left anterior descending artery

◆ *How does my heart work?*

The sinoatrial node starts an electric current that travels through the heart, setting off a contraction of the heart muscle. This contraction is called a heartbeat and is what pushes the blood out of the heart and sends it to the rest of your body. The sinoatrial node is located in the right upper chamber of the heart and is sometimes referred to as your heart's "natural pacemaker" since it is responsible for starting each heartbeat (Figure 1-4). Without this natural electrical system, the heart would not beat.

FIGURE 1-3. Artery inside and outside

Your heart pumps about 5 liters (~5 quarts) of blood per minute, a total of 1,800 gallons a day. It supplies oxygen and nutrients to the body. When you are resting, your heart beats an average of 60 to 80 beats per minute, which is over 100,000 times per day. Everyone's heart beats at a different rate, and yours may vary from the average depending on your overall physical condition, the type of heart problems you have experienced, and the medications you are currently using. Your resting heart rate is the

FIGURE 1-4. Heart showing sino-atrial node

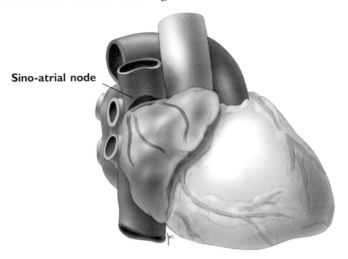

number of times your heart beats per minute while you are at rest. Ask your doctor about your normal resting heart rate.

◆ *How do I determine what my heart rate is?*

To check your heart rate, use your index and middle finger on one hand to trace the line of your thumb on the other hand. Trace the bone of your thumb down the side of your wrist. Just when you come to the line of your wrist, stop and then move your fingers slightly toward the middle of your wrist. In other words, you do not want to rest your fingers on the bone, but instead move them ever so slightly towards the palm of your hand (Figure 1-5). You should be able to feel your pulse at this location; it will feel like your wrist is bulging in and out just barely below your skin. The "bulging feeling" is your pulse. The feeling is actually the blood travelling through the artery to supply your hand with blood.

FIGURE 1-5. Taking a heart rate at the wrist

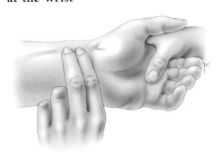

Once you feel your pulse, count the number of times it beats in 60 seconds. The easiest way to do this is to count the beats while watching a clock with a second hand on it. Remember to count the beats that you feel and not the seconds on the clock. The number of beats that you count in 60 seconds is your heart rate in "beats per minute." Although counting your pulse for 60 seconds is the most accurate way to determine your heart rate, sometimes it is not the most practical. For instance, counting your

TABLE 1-1. Ways to Count Your Pulse Rate

Count yourpulse for	Multiply by	Mathematical formula
6 seconds	10	No. of beats in 6 sec. × 10 = heart rate
10 seconds	6	No. of beats in 10 sec. × 6 = heart rate
15seconds	4	No. of beats in 15 sec. × 4 = heart rate
30 seconds	2	No. of beats in 30 sec. × 2 = heart rate
60 seconds	1	No. of beats in 60 sec. × 1 = heart rate

Source: Baylor Health Care System.

heart rate for 60 seconds while exercising may not give an accurate reading. By the time you stop, find your pulse, and count for a full minute, your heart rate may have already slowed down. There are several variations to counting your pulse rate (see Table 1-1).

Part 2

Cardiovascular Disease

Cardiovascular disease comes in many forms. Please talk to your doctor if you have any questions regarding different aspects of cardiovascular disease. Each person may have different symptoms than those defined in this book. Cardiovascular disease includes the following forms:

- Coronary Artery Disease
- Angina
- Myocardial Infarction (Heart Attack)
- Heart Valve Disorders
- Cardiomyopathy
- Congestive Heart Failure

- Peripheral Vascular Disease
- Cerebrovascular Accident (stroke/"Brain Attack")
- Abnormal Heart Rhythm

Coronary Artery Disease

Coronary artery disease is a lifelong process. It develops over many years, sometimes even starting in childhood. Coronary artery disease involves the increase of cholesterol within the walls of the coronary arteries, which leads to a plaque (atherosclerosis). Cholesterol is a type of fat. If there is too much cholesterol circulating in your blood, it sticks to the inside of your arteries. To understand the build up of

FIGURE 1-6. A partially clogged and clogged artery

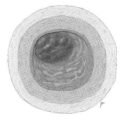

plaque, think of the substance that you try to control on your teeth to prevent tooth decay. Plaque is a sticky substance that builds up in arteries like it builds up on teeth.

The lumen (inside diameter) of the artery narrows as plaque forms within the walls of the artery (Figure 1-6). This reduces blood flow and decreases the delivery of blood and oxygen to the heart muscle. The result is similar to that of a clogged drainpipe. Over time, the narrowing may progress until the artery is completely blocked and will result in a heart attack.

Angina

Angina is the discomfort you feel when your heart muscle is not getting enough oxygen. Angina can be described as chest pain or pressure, sometimes radiating to the arms, back, jaw, or neck. You may also feel short of breath. Some people describe it as a feeling similar to indigestion. These are the most common symptoms of angina; however, you may have completely different symptoms. These symptoms, caused by narrowing of coronary arteries, may be mild or severe. Angina is a warning sign of coronary artery disease, but it does not necessarily cause permanent damage to the heart. It is usually relieved with rest or nitroglycerin. Nitroglycerin is a medication that helps to open up blood vessels, allowing blood and oxygen to reach the heart muscle. (For more information, refer to Chapter 2, Medications.)

If you think you may have angina, call your doctor. Do not wait. Depending on your symptoms, your doctor may want to see you immediately or ask you to go to the nearest emergency department.

Myocardial Infarction (Heart Attack)

When a narrowed artery becomes completely blocked, oxygen supply to the heart muscle is cut off. This results in a heart attack. The technical term for heart attack is myocardial infarction, which often leads to permanent damage to the heart muscle. A heart attack occurs when the plaque breaks open and a blood clot develops on top of the plaque, leading to complete blockage of the heart artery. Symptoms may include one or more of the following: angina, nausea and vomiting, sweating, indigestion, exhaustion, and a feeling of impending doom or "just not feeling right." If you have these symptoms, call 911 immediately.

Heart Valve Disorders

The heart has four valves that open and close to keep blood flowing in the proper direction (Figure 1-7). If the valves do not work properly, a valve will either become stopped up or it will leak. Common causes of valve problems are infections, birth defects, and the normal aging process. Be-

FIGURE 1-7. Open heart to show valves

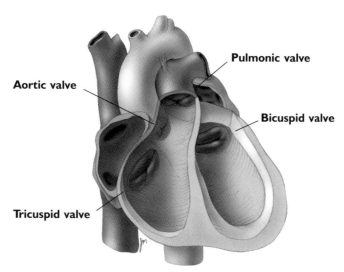

cause the blood is not flowing properly, symptoms of valve disorder may include shortness of breath, fatigue, and swollen ankles.

Cardiomyopathy

Cardiomyopathy is a form of cardiovascular disease in which the heart muscle may become enlarged resulting in a damaged and overall weak heart muscle. Possible causes of cardiomyopathy may be uncontrolled high blood pressure, viral illness, infection, or heavy alcohol consumption. Symptoms of cardiomyopathy may include fatigue, shortness of breath, and angina.

Congestive Heart Failure

Congestive heart failure is a condition in which the heart is unable to pump enough blood to provide good circulation; as a result, blood may back up into the lungs or legs. This may be caused by coronary artery disease, heart attack, high blood pressure, heart valve disorder, or cardiomyopathy. Symptoms of congestive heart failure may include shortness of breath, fatigue, unexplained weight gain, or fluid buildup throughout the body. A symptom of this type of fluid buildup would be extreme swelling in the legs or arms.

Peripheral Vascular Disease

Peripheral vascular disease is a condition in which the peripheral arteries become narrow or hardened. Peripheral arteries are responsible for delivering blood to the arms and legs. People with this disease have decreased blood flow in the arms and legs due to excessive plaque that has formed within the walls of the peripheral arteries. This condition is very similar to coronary artery disease. However, coronary artery disease affects the heart muscle, while peripheral vascular disease affects the blood vessels going to the legs or arms.

People with mild peripheral vascular disease often will not have symptoms if they are at rest. They may begin to feel muscle aching and cramping in the calf, thigh, or buttocks during exercise. Sometimes simply walking from a parking lot into a grocery store might be enough to trigger the start of symptoms. The aching and cramping may be severe enough that the person will have to sit down. This gradual aching, cramping, and pain is called claudication. In many people, claudication is minor, at first, and relieved by rest. As the disease becomes more severe, however, the person may begin to feel pain while sitting or even sleeping. Other symptoms of peripheral vascular disease may include change in skin color, tingling, numbness, or coldness, all of which will be in the arms and/or legs.

Cerebrovascular Accident (Stroke/"Brain Attack")

A stroke results from lack of oxygen to an area of the brain. It has several possible causes, one of which is blockage of an artery that supplies the brain with blood (similar to the blockage of a coronary artery). A stroke may occur without warning, or there may be symptoms leading to a stroke. The symptoms may include having trouble talking, feeling dizzy, having blurry vision, or being unable to move one side of the body. If you have these symptoms, call 911 immediately.

Abnormal Heart Rhythm

Any changes in the biological electrical system of the heart will result in an abnormal heart rhythm. For example, a heart rhythm may be too fast (tachycardia), too slow (bradycardia), or irregular (atrial fibrillation, atrial flutter, premature ventricular contraction, premature atrial contraction). An electrocardiogram (EKG) is a simple test that shows if your heart rhythm is abnormal (Figure 1-8).

FIGURE 1-8. A normal EKG

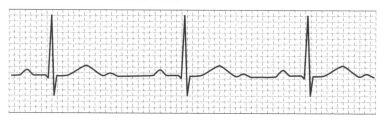

An abnormal heart rhythm could result from damaged muscle tissue (heart attack), congestive heart failure, stress, medicine, caffeine, nicotine, heart valve disorders, or illegal drug use. Symptoms may include fatigue, shortness of breath, chest pain, nausea, dizziness, or heart palpitations. Heart palpitations have been described as a fluttering feeling in the chest area.

Part 3

Risk Factors for Cardiovascular Disease

A risk factor is anything that increases your chances of developing a disease or condition. Risk factors may also cause the disease or condition to continue or worsen.

Cardiovascular disease risk factors are grouped into two types: controllable and uncontrollable. Controllable means you have a choice in changing these risk factors. For example, you make the decision to smoke or not to smoke. The controllable risk factors for cardiovascular disease are tobacco use, lipid levels, exercise, body weight, blood pressure, and diabetes. Uncontrollable risk factors are those you are unable to change, such as your age. The uncontrollable risk factors are age, gender, and family history. Sometimes if you change one controllable risk factor you might improve your other risk factors. For example, if you decrease your body weight, you might also lower your blood pressure. The following paragraphs will explain each risk factor and give you tools to manage the ones that affect you.

Controllable Risk Factors

Tobacco

Tobacco use and exposure to secondhand smoke can increase your risk of cardiovascular disease by damaging artery walls and thickening the blood. All forms of tobacco, not just cigarettes, contain nicotine. Nicotine causes blood vessels to constrict and increases blood pressure and heart rate, which can lead to atherosclerosis. Cigarette smoke contains carbon monoxide. When carbon monoxide is inhaled, the amount of available oxygen to the heart and body will decrease.

Additional components are included in tobacco products, the effects of which are still unknown. No matter how much or how long you have smoked, once you quit smoking your risk of cardiovascular disease drops (Figure 1-9). By quitting cigarette smoking, the risk of another heart attack or death from cardiovascular disease is decreased by 50% (American Heart Association). Remember, it is never too late to quit.

To better manage this risk factor:

- Research the different methods available to help you stop using tobacco.
- Talk with your family and friends and let them know your plan.
- Talk to your doctor about medications that may help you quit.
- Decrease the amount of tobacco you use.
- Set a quit date—and quit.
- Discuss the use of nicotine replacement therapy with your doctor.
- Avoid exposure to second-hand smoke.
- Consider chewing sugarless gum.
- Consider a tobacco cessation book or local program to help you quit.
- Change your social gatherings to those that do not encourage tobacco use.

FIGURE 1-9.

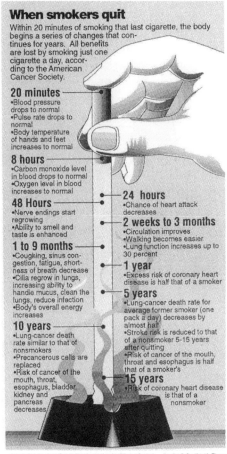

When smokers quit

Within 20 minutes of smoking that last cigarette, the body begins a series of changes that continues for years. All benefits are lost by smoking just one cigarette a day, according to the American Cancer Society.

20 minutes
•Blood pressure drops to normal
•Pulse rate drops to normal
•Body temperature of hands and feet increases to normal

8 hours
•Carbon monoxide level in blood drops to normal
•Oxygen level in blood increases to normal

48 Hours
•Nerve endings start regrowing
•Ability to smell and taste is enhanced

1 to 9 months
•Coughing, sinus congestion, fatigue, shortness of breath decrease
•Cilia regrow in lungs, increasing ability to handle mucus, clean the lungs, reduce infection
•Body's overall energy increases

10 years
•Lung-cancer death rate similar to that of nonsmokers
•Precancerous cells are replaced
•Risk of cancer of the mouth, throat, esophagus, bladder, kidney and pancreas decreases

24 hours
•Chance of heart attack decreases

2 weeks to 3 months
•Circulation improves
•Walking becomes easier
•Lung function increases up to 30 percent

1 year
•Excess risk of coronary heart disease is half that of a smoker

5 years
•Lung-cancer death rate for average former smoker (one pack a day) decreases by almost half
•Stroke risk is reduced to that of a nonsmoker 5-15 years after quitting
•Risk of cancer of the mouth, throat and esophagus is half that of a smoker's

15 years
•Risk of coronary heart disease is that of a nonsmoker

Source: The American Cancer Society, Centers for Disease Control   Randee S. Fox/Seattle Times

Lipid levels

You may have been told you need to have a blood test for a "lipid profile," but what does that mean? A lipid is a particle in the body that is greasy or oily. Since lipid is a fancy word for a fat molecule, a lipid profile is a way of measuring the different types of fats in your blood. Two types of lipids are found in your blood: triglycerides and cholesterol.

Cholesterol is a type of lipid that helps give structure to the cell membranes.

Cholesterol plays an important role in the development of cell walls and hormones. However, when there is too much cholesterol in your bloodstream, it can stick to the walls of your arteries and be a factor in the development of atherosclerosis.

Cholesterol travels in the blood in "packages" called lipoproteins. A lipoprotein is formed by combining a protein and a lipid. Lipoproteins carry lipids around the body by way of the blood. Some are high-density lipoproteins (HDL) and others are low-density lipoproteins (LDL).

An HDL, which is sometimes called "good cholesterol," is formed by the combination of a large amount of protein with a small amount of lipid. Proteins weigh more than lipids. That's why this molecule is called high-density lipoprotein. A high HDL level is good to have since HDL helps prevent plaque formation by removing cholesterol from the bloodstream (the protein in the HDL attaches to the wall of the arteries and removes the excess cholesterol).

An LDL, which is often referred to as "bad cholesterol," is formed by the combination of a small amount of protein and a large amount of cholesterol. High levels of LDL increase the risk of developing atherosclerosis, since the protein in this molecule attaches to the cell wall in the artery and deposits cholesterol. Lipids are less dense than proteins, so this molecule is called a low-density lipoprotein since it has more lipid than protein.

Your body makes triglycerides every time you eat. Triglycerides are essential to the human body since they are used for energy. Triglycerides are either used as energy or deposited in the body as fat cells. High triglyceride levels may result when you consume too many calories, drink alcohol, and/or eat foods high in sugar. Being overweight may also increase your triglyceride level. When your triglyceride level is too high you have a greater risk of developing problems like diabetes, high blood pressure, and increased amounts of blood cholesterol. Since high triglyceride levels may lead to increased blood cholesterol, the risk for cardiovascular disease also increases.

> **"All these people who just say, 'Well, you ought to quit.' Well, it's not that easy."**
>
> *Heart attack survivor—has not smoked for seven months*

◆ What is the difference between triglycerides and cholesterol?

Both triglycerides and cholesterol are essential for life. Cholesterol is used in the body for cell structure; triglycerides are used for energy.

There are two ways for cholesterol to get into our system:

- The body produces its own.
- Certain foods provide it.

Triglycerides are formed in the body after you eat sugar and saturated fat. Triglycerides are also formed by overeating and taking in more food than can be used for energy. When a person eats too much saturated fat, the body can increase its blood cholesterol by as much as 15% to 25% (Guyton, 1981).

◆ Is there anything I need to do before I have my lipid profile test?

Different factors affect blood levels of cholesterol and triglycerides. These include exercise, drugs, a recent heart attack, stroke, trauma, illness, and recent food intake. For these reasons, you will want to ask your doctor for specific instructions before getting your lipids measured. Your doctor may give guidelines similar to those following, depending on your specific medical need:

- Try to keep your weight consistent. Avoid dieting or weight gain for two weeks.
- Wait at least eight weeks after a heart attack, stroke, illness, or trauma.
- Do not eat for 12 hours before the test (other than water and prescribed medications).
- Do not exercise for at least 12 hours before the test.

◆ *What is considered a good lipid profile value?*

Table 1-2 shows recommended values for your lipid profile. Please discuss the recommendations and possible options to improve your lipid levels with your doctor.

TABLE 1-2. Recommended Values for Your Lipid Profile.

Total Cholesterol	HDL
• Desirable = less than 200 mg/dL • Borderline-high = 200 to 239 mg/dL • High = 240 mg/dL and over	• Goal = greater than 35 mg/dL • An HDL of 60 mg/dL or above is considered to protect you against cardiovascular disease
Triglyceride	**LDL**
• Normal = less than 200 mg/dL • Borderline-high = 200 to 400 mg/dL • High = 400 to 1000 mg/dL • Very high = greater than 1000 mg/dL	• Desirable = less than 130 mg/dL • Borderline-high = 130 to 159 mg/dL • High = 160 mg/dL and over • Goal = less than 100mg/dL if you have cardiovascular disease

Source: National Heart, Lung and Blood Institute and the American Heart Association

◆ *What is a cholesterol ratio?*

You may have heard of something called a cholesterol ratio or coronary risk ratio. This is the ratio of your total cholesterol to your HDL value. Although it is good to know your cholesterol ratio, since the cholesterol ratio is a general number, it is also important to know the values of each lipid profile level. To determine your cholesterol ratio, use the following formula:

$$\frac{\text{Total cholesterol}}{\text{HDL}} = \text{Cholesterol ratio}$$

For example, if Julie's total cholesterol is 230 mg/dL and her HDL is 65 mg/dL, the calculation for Julie's cholesterol ratio would look like this:

$$\frac{230 \text{ mg/dL}}{65 \text{ mg/dL}} = 3.5$$

According to the American Heart Association, the goal for a cholesterol ratio is 5.0 and the ideal value is 3.5. Figure 1-10 is a tear-out card on which you can record your cholesterol and blood pressure values.

◈ *I have heard about advanced lipid testing. What is it?*

It is surprising that 80% of patients with coronary artery disease have the same lipid profile as the general population (Dawber, 1980). There are other inherited factors that affect lipids, and, if not tested for routinely, these factors may triple the risk of a heart attack or other coronary event.

The good news is that these genetic abnormalities can now be measured using advanced laboratory techniques. Today, these abnormalities can be detected, and, if detected, they can be treated, resulting in a reduced risk of cardiovascular disease.

The results of normal lipid testing, such as total cholesterol, HDL, LDL, and triglyceride measurements, are important. However, for those individuals with a personal or family history of heart attack, new, advanced testing is suggested by the American College of Cardiology and the American Heart Association.

◈ *What does the advanced testing measure?*

LDL-GGE, or LDL particle concentration, is a direct measurement of the LDL particle size or concentration. While the calculated LDL is used in a normal lipid profile, the calculated LDL measurement does not tell anything about the size of the LDL particles that make up the overall LDL volume. The size of the numerous types of LDL particles is important because small, dense LDL particles (Pattern B) settle between the cells in the artery wall more easily than large, buoyant LDL particles (Pattern A). Medications are available that actually convert small, dense LDL particles into the less harmful large, fluffy, and buoyant LDL particles. Knowing your specific LDL type assists your doctor in prescribing the right treatment plan for you.

Lipoprotein A is a "tail" that is sometimes found on LDL particles. The tail appears to "hook" the LDL into the artery wall more easily, causing additional LDL particle buildup and a higher risk of atherosclerosis and heart attack. The presence of lipoprotein A is genetically predisposed; in other words, it is something that is part of your genetic makeup. A specific medication can help change this genetic structure.

Homocysteine is an amino acid (protein) in the blood. A high level of homocysteine is a risk factor for cardiovascular disease. About 20% to 30% of persons who have cardiovascular disease also have elevated levels of homocysteine. The tendency to have elevated homocysteine is inherited; therefore, elevated homocysteine is looked for in persons with a family history of cardiovascular disease. Specific vitamins can be prescribed to reduce homocysteine levels.

◆ *Is advanced lipid testing right for me?*

You and your doctor can determine if advanced lipid testing is right for you. If you have questions about the testing, ask your doctor.

To better manage this risk factor:

- Talk to your doctor.
- Eat less saturated fat and sugar.
- Drink less alcohol.
- Exercise.
- Stop using tobacco.
- Know your lipid profile values.

Exercise

In July 1996, the U.S. Surgeon General reported that exercise is vital for good health. Exercise can help strengthen your heart muscle, burn calories, control your blood sugar, lower your blood pressure, raise your HDL levels, reduce stress, and help you to lose weight. To learn more about how to plan a proper exercise program, turn to Chapter 3 in this book.

To better manage this risk factor:

- Ask your doctor when it is safe for you to begin an exercise program.
- Set a start date for your exercise program and stick to it.
- Start slowly, do not try to exercise every day of the week if you are not used to exercising regularly.
- Find ways to be more active in your daily life. For example, take the stairs instead of the elevator or park away from the mall door and walk a greater distance.

REMOVE FROM BOOK ALONG PERFORATION

Figure 1-10. Lipids, Blood Pressure and Medication Card

Name ______________________ Doctor(s) ______________________

My phone number ______________________ My doctors' phone numbers ______________________

Lipids	Total Cholesterol	LDL	HDL	Triglyceride	Ratio
Date:					
Date:					
Date:					
Date:					

Blood Pressure	Value		Value		Value
Date:	/	Date:	/	Date:	/
Date:	/	Date:	/	Date:	/
Date:	/	Date:	/	Date:	/
Date:	/	Date:	/	Date:	/
Date:	/	Date:	/	Date:	/
Date:	/	Date:	/	Date:	/

See reverse side.

Medications

Date:

Name	Dose	Why I Take It	Name	Dose	Why I Take It

Body Weight

If you weigh too much, you may also have high body fat content. Although some fat is necessary to protect organs, fat is an inactive tissue to which your heart must pump blood. Having a lot of body fat means extra work for your heart, which can result in a higher heart rate and/or blood pressure. Think of your heart as a sprinkler system and your body as the yard which needs to be watered. If you have just one sprinkler that must water a large yard, the water pressure will have to be turned very high to reach the far corners. If, however, your yard is small, the same sprinkler will be able to water the yard more effectively while using less water pressure. In other words, as your body fat increases, your heart has to beat harder and faster to supply the extra fat with blood.

Body mass index is one way to determine if you are overweight or underweight. (This body mass index table is graphically represented in Table 4-1.) Although being underweight is not a risk factor for cardiovascular disease, having too little fat can lead to bone loss and other health problems.

To better manage this risk factor:

- Ask your doctor what a healthful body mass index is for you.
- Ask your doctor how to achieve the level if it is different from where you are right now.
- Eat out less.
- Be more active.
- Know your ideal body weight.
- Schedule an appointment with a licensed dietitian if needed.
- Review Chapter 4 of this book.

Blood Pressure

Blood pressure is the force of blood pushing against the walls of the arteries. The ideal blood pressure reading is 120/80 mm/Hg (Table 1-3 shows blood pressure ranges). Your blood pressure changes throughout the day depending on a number of factors, but a blood pressure that is

TABLE 1-3. Blood Pressure Ranges

For adults age 18 or older:

- "Optimal" blood pressure is defined as less than 120/80 mm/Hg while "normal" blood pressure is less than 130/85 mm/Hg.
- "High normal" blood pressure is 130-139/85-89 mm/Hg.
- "High" blood pressure is anything over 140/90 mm/Hg.

Source: National Heart, Lung and Blood Institute, 1999.

above 140/90 most of the time is considered high. The technical term for high blood pressure is hypertension. High blood pressure is sometimes referred to as the "silent killer" since for the most part you cannot feel changes in your blood pressure; therefore, it might be dangerously high while you are unaware of it. This could be dangerous to your health and is why it is especially important to have your blood pressure checked regularly. For most people, there is no single known cause of high blood pressure. However, medications can effectively control it. For more information, see Chapter 2.

> **Did you know that high blood pressure is more common in African Americans than Caucasians? High blood pressure often occurs earlier in life and is more severe in African Americans.**
>
> *American Heart Association, 2000*

Some people have a blood pressure that is below 120/80 most of the time. This does not increase your risk of having cardiovascular disease. Since every person's blood pressure is slightly different, talk to your doctor to find out what your blood pressure should be.

To better manage this risk factor:

- Talk to your doctor.
- Regularly monitor your blood pressure and know the values.
- Stay at a healthy weight.
- Eat less salt.
- Exercise.
- Drink less alcohol.

Diabetes Mellitus

> **Did you know that in the year 2000 diabetes is so common in the Native American communities that it has become an epidemic?**
>
> *Amercian Diabetes Association, 2000*

Diabetes is a condition in which the body is not able to move glucose (sugar) from blood into its cells to be used for energy. Diabetes causes changes in your arteries that increase your risk for developing cardiovascular disease. Table 1-4 is a risk assessment for diabetes that was created by the American Diabetes Association. Take time to fill out the information in Table 1-4 and talk to your doctor if you think you may be at risk.

TABLE 1-4. Are You at Risk for Developing Diabetes?

Instructions: Take the test below to see if you are at risk for developing diabetes. If the answer to the question is yes, circle the number after the equal sign. For example, Yes = 5. If yes, circle 5. After you answer all seven questions, add the numbers you circled to get the total score. Read the box at the bottom to see what your score means.

Answer these questions ...	Yes?
My weight is equal to or above that listed in the height/weight chart (on the following page)	Yes = 5
I am under 65 years of age AND get little or no exercise during the usual day	Yes = 5
I am between 45 and 64 years of age	Yes = 5
I am 65 years old or older	Yes = 9
I am a woman who has had a baby weighing more than nine pounds at birth	Yes = 1
I have a sister or a brother with diabetes	Yes = 1
I have a parent with diabetes	Yes = 1
Total Score:	

Scoring 3–9 points:
You are probably at low risk for having diabetes now. But don't just forget about it—especially if you are Hispanic, African American, American Indian, Asian American, or Pacific Islander. You may be at higher risk in the future. New guidelines recommend everyone age 40 and older should consider being tested for the disease every three years. However, people at high risk should consider being tested at a younger age.

Scoring 10 or more points:
You are at high risk for having diabetes. Only a doctor can determine if you have diabetes. See a doctor soon and find out for sure.

TABLE 1-4. (continued)

Height (without shoes)	Weight (without clothes)
4'10"	129
4'11"	133
5'0"	138
5'1"	143
5'2"	147
5'3"	152
5'4"	157
5'5"	162
5'6"	167
5'7"	172
5'8"	177
5'9"	182
5'10"	188
5'11"	193
6'0"	199
6'1"	204
6'2"	210
6'3"	216
6'4"	221

If you weigh the same or more than the amount listed for your height, you may be at risk for diabetes. This chart is based on a measure called the Body Mass Index (BMI). It shows unhealthful weight for men and women, age 35 or older, at listed heights. At-risk weights are lower for individuals under age 35.

To better manage this risk factor:
- Talk to your doctor.
- Know your blood sugar levels.
- Keep your blood sugar under control.
- Manage your weight.
- Exercise regularly.
- Follow a healthful diet.

Uncontrollable Risk Factors

Age

Men 45 years or older and women 55 years or older are at higher risk for developing cardiovascular disease. Also, women who have passed menopause or have had their ovaries and uterus surgically removed and are not taking estrogen are considered at greater risk for developing cardiovascular disease regardless of their age (American Heart Association).

Gender

Research has shown men to be at higher risk than women, although cardiovascular disease is still the number one killer of both genders (American Heart Association).

Family History

You are at higher risk if your father or brother had cardiovascular disease before age 55 or your mother or sister had it before age 65. Studies are being conducted to explore certain substances and/or genes in the body that occur in families and are linked to a high frequency of cardiovascular disease.

Risk factors such as high blood pressure, high cholesterol, and diabetes are health issues that can cause you to have a greater chance of developing cardiovascular disease. In order to decrease your risk of cardiovascular disease, it is important to know your controllable risk factors and change them.

2

Common Heart Medications

It is important to know what medications you are taking, why you are taking them, and how they affect your health. Some medications play a very important role in controlling diseases and curing infections and may only need to be taken for a short period of time. Other medications may help your body work better than it does on its own and may need to be taken over a lifetime. If your doctor has prescribed a medication for you, it is important to your body, and you need to take it as prescribed. After reading this section, you should have a general understanding of your medications.

The questions and answers in this section will give you important information about many cardiovascular medications; however, there are three main recommendations. First, do not stop taking any medication just because you feel better without first checking with your doctor. Second, do not take extra doses of a medication without checking with your doctor. Third, if you have been taking a medicine and you "just do not feel right," it is time to call your doctor.

Part I
Common Information

◆ *Should I keep a list of all my medications?*

You should keep a list of your medications with you at all times. This list should include the following information:

- Names of all your medications, including prescriptions, vitamins, and medicines that do not require a doctor's prescription (such as aspirin or cough medicine).
- Amount of each medicine (for example, 125-milligram tablet).
- How often you take the medicine.

- The name and telephone number of the doctor who prescribed the medication for you.
- Names of medications that you are allergic to.
- The name and number of your primary care or family doctor for reference.

Figure 1-10 (Chapter 1) provides you with a perforated card to complete your information. This list can provide medical professionals with important information in case you are in an accident or for some reason are not able to communicate. This list will also help medical professionals

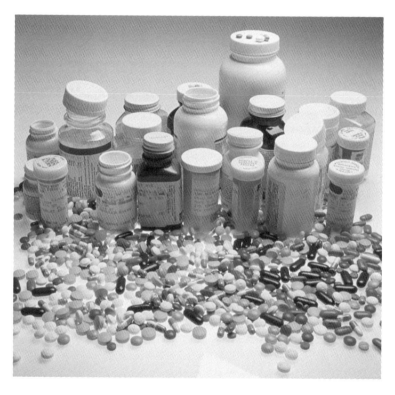

keep track of what medications you are taking. To keep your doctors, dentists, pharmacists, and any other health professionals informed of your medications, make them aware of your list at each office visit. Remember to update this list whenever your doctor changes your medications in any way. Also, do not forget to write down any changes in the medicines you take that do not require a doctor's prescription (for example, vitamins and allergy medicine).

◆ Why should I get all my prescriptions filled at the same pharmacy?

A pharmacy must keep records of all your prescriptions for five years. This record is very important and includes medications you are currently taking as well as medications you took in the past. It is referred to every time you get a refill or have a new prescription filled. This list is especially important if you have more than one doctor prescribing medications for you or if you do not carry a list of your current medications to the doctor with you each time you go. The pharmacist can double-check your record to make sure that:

- You are not taking two medications that are the same but have different names (for example, one is the name brand and one is the generic name).
- There are no dangerous drug interactions (for example, you are on two medications that are safe when used alone but dangerous when put together).
- You are not allergic to any medications prescribed to you.

If it is not possible for you to use only one pharmacy, bring your updated list of medications with you each time you fill a prescription so that the information can be added to your record. Always verify your list with the pharmacy list to make sure both are current and accurate and, remember to order refills a few days before you run out of medication so that you do not skip a dose.

◆ What questions should I ask my doctor about new medications that I am going to take?

When a new medication has been prescribed for you, you may want to ask your doctor, nurse or pharmacist the following questions about it:

- Why am I taking this medicine?
- When do I need to take this medication?
- When is the best time of day to take this medication?
- Do I need to take this medicine with or without food?
- What are the side effects?
- If I think I am having any of the side effects, what should I do?
- Does this new medicine affect any of the medicines I am already on?
- Does my insurance cover this medication?
- Is there a generic brand for this medicine? Can I take the generic brand?
- How long will I take this medicine?

◆ What if I forget to take my medication?

When a new medicine is prescribed for you, talk with your doctor and/or pharmacist about what to do if you miss a dose. If this is a common problem for you, you may want to keep a journal or wear a wristwatch with an alarm to remind yourself when to take the medicine.

Some general guidelines to follow are:

- Never double-up on doses unless instructed to do so by your doctor or pharmacist.
- Never stop taking any of your medicine without first asking your doctor—even if you start to feel better.

◆ Where should I store my medications?

Where do you think is the best place to store your medications? If you look at Table 2-1 and give the answer that dark, cool, dry, motionless areas are the best places to store medications, you are right. Always remember to keep all medications out of the reach of children; locked areas are the safest.

Hot temperatures can make medicine less effective or even harmful. For this reason, the cabinets above and around the stove and oven are not good storage spaces for your medications. Moisture can also cause medications to lose effectiveness. Therefore, areas near the dishwasher, sink, bathroom, and refrigerator are not good storage areas for medications.

Light is also harmful to a number of medications. Therefore, avoid the windowsill as a storage area for your medicine. Drawers may seem like a good storage area since they are dark and dry, but every time a drawer is

TABLE 2-1. Storage Areas for Medications.

Storage Area	Yes/No	Why?
Locked cabinet away from heat and humidity	YES	Cool, dry, locked, and motionless
Small cabinet above the stove or oven	NO	Too hot
Kitchen counter above the dishwasher	NO	Too hot and moist
Kitchen windowsill	NO	Too much light
Desk, kitchen, or bathroom drawer	NO	Pills bump together
Bathroom medicine cabinet	NO	Too hot and moist

Source: Baylor Health Care System.

opened and closed the pills bump together. This can damage coated tablets, so that they may not work properly, and also cause non-coated tablets to crack and crumble.

What if I cannot afford the medication that is prescribed for me?

If your doctor puts you on a medication that you cannot afford, tell your doctor immediately. This is much better than simply not getting the prescription filled. Your doctor is assuming that you will fill the prescription that was written for you and will not know that you are not taking the medicine due to the expense. With the number of medications available today, there may be something that works just as well for you but costs less. In summary, it is important to let your doctor know if a medicine is too expensive for you.

How should I handle my medications when traveling?

If you are traveling by car, keep your medications on the seat beside you or on the back seat out of direct sunlight. Do not store medications on the floorboard or in the trunk, since these places may become quite hot on long trips. If traveling by airplane, ask your pharmacist to give you an extra storage bottle so that you can split your medication between the two containers. Keep one bottle with you and one in your luggage. If your luggage gets delayed or your purse gets stolen, you will have an extra bottle. Before you leave for a trip, count your pills to see if you have enough to last. If not, ask the pharmacist to refill your medication before you leave.

Where should I keep my nitroglycerin tablets?

If you take nitroglycerin, remember that it must be kept with you at all times and within a quick, easy reach. Since light, heat, and moisture may damage or decompose nitroglycerin, it must be protected and kept in its original, dark container. A pants or dress pocket is not a good place to keep your nitroglycerin since your body temperature is high enough to be harmful to the medication. In general, your front shirt pocket, jacket pocket, or purse is the best place to keep your bottle of nitroglycerin tablets or your nitroglycerin spray. These areas keep the medicine from being kept too tightly against the body. If, however, you will be outside in the heat for a prolonged period of time, you will want to keep your nitroglycerin close at hand, but not in your pocket or purse. Consider leaving it just inside the door of an air-conditioned area so that you can get to it quickly if needed.

Part 2

Common Cardiovascular Medications

◆ *How do common heart medications work?*

It may help you to understand what actions your heart medications have on your heart muscle and your body. Some medications may cause your heart to beat stronger, while others make it easier for your heart to pump blood. When your heart rate is high, your heart is working harder and it needs more oxygen. When your heart rate is low, your heart is not working as hard and, therefore, needs less oxygen. For example:

- Increased heart rate = Increased workload on the heart and increased need for oxygen
- Decreased heart rate = Decreased workload on the heart and decreased need for oxygen

Medications of each classification are listed with the brand name followed by the ® symbol. The generic name is in parentheses next to the brand name. The medication list is complete as of the time of publication, but new medications are constantly being approved. Please ask your doctor or pharmacist about a medication that is not included in this book.

ACE Inhibitors

Common examples:

Accupril® (quinapril)
Altace® (ramipril)
Capoten® (captopril)
Lotensin® (benazepril)
Lotensin HCT® (benazepril & HCTZ)
Lotrel® (benazepril & amlodipine)

Mavik® (trandolapril)
Monopril® (fosinopril)
Prinivil® (lisinopril)
Univasc® (moexipril)
Vasotec® (enalapril)
Zestril® (lisinopril)

ACE inhibitors block enzymes involved in certain chemical reactions in your body that constrict your blood vessels. Simply stated, blocking the enzymes helps to lower blood pressure and can increase the heart's ability to pump blood.

Angiotensin II Receptor Antagonists

Common examples:

Atacand® (candesartan)
Avapro® (irbesartan)

Cozaar® (losartan)
Diovan® (valsartan)

Hyzaar® (losartan, HCTZ)   Tevetan® (eprosartan)
Micardis® (telmisartan)

These drugs allow your blood vessels to dilate (get bigger) and help your kidneys to get rid of extra sodium and water. These two actions work together to help lower blood pressure, and may also increase the heart's ability to pump blood.

Antiarrhythmics

Common examples:

Betapace® (sotalol)   Procanbid® (procainamide)
Cordarone® (amiodarone)   Quinidine®
Ethmozine® (moricizine)   Rythmol® (propafenone)
Lanoxin® (digoxin)   Tambocor® (flecainide)
Norpace® (disopyramide)

Antiarrhythmic drugs are used to control irregular heart rhythms. The medication helps the heart contract in a normal pattern.

Anticoagulants and Antiplatelets

Common examples:

Coumadin® (warfarin)   Lovenox® (enoxaparin)
Fragmin® (dalteparin)   Plavix® (clopidogrel)
Heparin® injection   Ticlid® (ticlopidine)

Harmful blood clots can cause many problems, including stroke and heart attack. Anticoagulant drugs help prevent the formation of new blood clots and also help prevent them from getting bigger. Antiplatelets keep blood clots from forming by making the platelets (a part of the blood that is involved in making the clot) work less. Anticoagulants and/or antiplatelets are usually used after an angioplasty, heart attack, or valve surgery and/or for abnormal heart rhythms.

Beta-Blockers

Common examples:

Betapace® (sotalol)   Normodyne®, Trandate® (labetalol)
Corgard® (naldolol)   Sectral® (acebutolol)
Inderal® (propranolol)   Tenormin® (atenolol)
Kerlon® (betaxolol)   Visken® (pindolol)
Levatol® (penbutolol)   Ziac® (bisoprolol & HCTZ)
Lopressor® (metoprolol)

Beta-blockers decrease the heart rate and generally make it easier for the heart to pump. They lower your blood pressure and decrease the work of the heart. Beta-blockers can be used to treat high blood pressure, angina, and abnormal rhythms of the heart.

Calcium Channel Blockers

Common examples:

Adalat®, Adalat CC®, Procardia®, Procardia XL® (nifedipine)
Calan, Calan SR®, Covera®, Sioptin®, IsoptinSR®, Verelan® (verapamil)
Cardene®, Cardene SR® (nicardipine)
Cardizem®, Cardizem Sr® and CD®, Dilacor XR®, Tiazac® (diltiazem)
Dynacirc® (isradipine)
Nimotop® (nimodipine)
Norvasc® (amlodipine)
Plendil® (felodipine)
Posicor® (mibenfradil)
Sular® (nisoldipine)
Vasocor® (bepridil)

These drugs "block" muscle contraction and nerve impulses in the heart. Not all calcium channel blockers work the same way. Some calcium channel blockers dilate arteries (make the inside of the artery bigger), increase or decrease heart rate, slow the ability of the heart to contract, and slow nerve impulse conduction through the heart. Some are used to treat irregular heartbeats, and others are used to treat angina. Calcium channel blockers do not affect calcium levels in the blood or calcium use in the bones.

Digoxin

Common examples:

Lanoxicaps® (digoxin)   Lanoxin® (digoxin)

Digoxin increases the amount of calcium inside the cells of the heart and causes the heart muscle to beat stronger. Digoxin is most commonly used to reduce the symptoms of heart failure (caused by a weak heart muscle). It also may be used to control certain types of abnormal heart rhythms.

Diuretics

Common examples:

Aldactazide® (spironolactone/hydrochlorothiazide)
Aldactone® (spironolactone)

Bumex® (bumetanide)
Demadex® (torsemide)
Diuril® (chlorothiazide)
HydroDIURIL®, Oretic® (hydrochlorothiazide)
Lasix® (furosemide)
Lozol® (indapamide)
Maxzide®, Dyazide® (triamterene/hydrochlorothiazide)
Zaroxolyn® (metolazone)

Diuretics cause the kidneys to expel more sodium and water than usual. A symptom of fluid buildup throughout the body is excessive swelling in legs or arms. Diuretics take extra fluid that is not being utilized by your body out of your tissues, which increases the amount of urine you have. This process will most likely cause you to go to the bathroom more often than usual. Diuretics are most commonly used to treat high blood pressure and fluid retention (including fluid retention due to heart failure).

Lipid-Lowering Medications

Common examples:

Atromid-S® (clofibrate)
Baycol® (cerivastatin)
Cholybar®, Prevalite®,
Questran® (cholestyramine)
Colestid® (colestipol)
Lescol® (fluvastatin)
Lipitor® (atorvastatin)

Lopid® (gemfibrizol)
Lorelco® (probucol)
Mevacor® (lovastatin)
Pravachol® (pravastatin)
Tricor® (fenofibrate)
Zocor® (simvastatin)

There are several different classes of lipid-lowering medications, and each class may work a little differently from the others. These drugs may reduce the production of low-density lipoprotein, which is associated with narrowing of the arteries and increased risk of heart or blood vessel disease. In some cases these drugs may lower total cholesterol and triglyceride levels in the blood or even raise high-density lipoprotein levels. Ask your doctor or pharmacist for a more detailed description of what your lipid-lowering medication does.

Nitrates

Common examples:
Dilitrate®
Imdur®
Ismo®, Amyl Nitrate (inhalant)

Isordil®
Monoket®
Nitroglycerin (sprays, tablets, capsules, ointment, and patches)
Sorbitrate®

Nitrates are used for the treatment of angina. They are available for short- or long-term use. The short-term products relieve immediate pain—for example, if your angina is not a constant pain but instead hurts every once in a while. Examples of short-term nitrates are the tablets and sprays that go under your tongue, inhalants, and chewable tablets. The long-term products are used to prevent angina that is constant over long periods of time.

The nitroglycerin tablets and spray that go under your tongue should be replaced with a new supply six months after the bottle has been opened. Nitroglycerin may sting when placed under the tongue.

If you use nitroglycerin patches, it is important to rotate where you place the patch each time you use one. This will help prevent skin irritation. Do not try to treat skin irritation with lotions or ointments. Instead, call your doctor or pharmacist.

3

Active Living

What is it like to have a heart attack? The experience is different for everyone. In August 1999 Jackie's life changed forever. That summer Jackie started to notice a pain in her chest that she thought was indigestion. She called her doctor and he told her to come see him that week for an electrocardiogram (EKG) to check her heart rhythm. The day of her appointment the doctor was concerned with her EKG results. He told Jackie he was making an appointment for her later that day to get an echocardiogram test that would show a better picture of her heart. To have this next test done, Jackie would have to drive to the hospital that was not far from her home. The appointment was scheduled for later that afternoon, so Jackie went home first to call her boss since she knew she would be late for work. After a few hours, she drove herself to the hospital for the echocardiogram.

This is the part that gets cloudy when Jackie is telling her story. She does not remember many things about that second test. In fact, her memory is based on what her doctors and her family have told her. As it turns out, she began having a heart attack during the echocardiogram test. Shortly after the heart attack and as soon as she was out of immediate danger, her doctors made the decision to send her to a larger hospital in a nearby city that would be better able to handle her treatment. Her doctors also decided that due to the possibility of heavy rush-hour traffic, which could very easily change the 30 mile drive into a two-hour ordeal, she would be taken by medical helicopter.

Shortly after the helicopter trip, Jackie had another test to determine which artery on her heart was blocked and had caused the heart attack. The doctors were able to see which one it was, so they placed a stent in the artery to increase the blood flow to her heart. Jackie remained in the hospital for four days. For an entire month after she came home from the hospital, she continued to have angina (chest pain) symptoms and was taking medication to relieve the pain. Since the chest pain did not go away, her doctor put two more stents in her heart. Although she does not remember much about the first procedure in the hospital to implant the stent, she says waiting for the second one was difficult. She knew what it would be like since she already had one stent; all she had to do now was wait. "That was a tough time for me. Just to go in cold turkey and know what you were going to have done."

Many people with cardiovascular disease have a hospital experience similar to Jackie's. After such a life-changing event, the questions remain the same for everyone: "Now what?" "How do I live with cardiovascular disease?" The good news is that there are many options for the millions of people living with cardiovascular disease that will help them lead healthy, normal lives.

Jackie began cardiac rehabilitation about a month after her heart attack. Rehabilitation classes were held three days a week, and although she couldn't attend every session, she completed the class. She now plans to join a local fitness center, which is in the same building as the cardiac rehabilitation department. She states, "I thought it would be good for me to stay in that routine at least for awhile. I can tell my strength has come back."

Jackie continues to exercise at least three days each week and has set goals to keep herself motivated to stay healthy. She is especially proud of the fact that she has not touched a cigarette since the day of her heart attack. "My main goal that I have stuck to and hope and pray that I continue is that I stopped smoking. I haven't smoked since that day on the way to the hospital." She does say that the healthier she gets, the more she wants a cigarette, but she tries "to think not only for myself, but what all my family has done to try to help me quit," and that keeps her going each day.

Part I

Activity: Why Not?

If a pill were created that would help you lose weight, have more energy, strengthen your bones, help you sleep better, and control your cholesterol, blood pressure, and risk for cardiovascular disease, would you take it? Most likely, if research showed that this drug was safe to take, many of us would jump at the chance to have this "wonder pill." Much of society is trying desperately to find this fictitious remedy without realizing that a regular exercise program will provide all the benefits listed above plus many more.

That's right, exercise. That dreaded eight-letter word that we would rather refer to as lifestyle activity. It sounds better already, and what is even better is that studies have shown that on average people who are physically active outlive those who are not (Centers for Disease Control, U.S. Department of Health and Human Services).

Why, then, do many people choose not to live an active life? With all the current news stories related to the benefits of exercise and activity, it is surprising to realize that in 1996, 60% of the American population reported not being regularly active and 25% reported not being active at all (U.S. Department of Health and Human Services). These numbers are in spite of the fact that many popular news magazines and television shows frequently feature stories on the benefits of activity. People are aware of the benefits yet do not take advantage of them. Why?

Many people believe that if they are not able to run a certain amount of miles each day, they might as well not do anything. It is now known that the "no pain, no gain," high-intensity exercising that was popular in the early 1980s is not necessary for good health. This chapter will discuss current recommendations for leading an active lifestyle. You might be surprised to learn that more is not necessarily better.

Part 2
Why?

Take a minute to reflect on your average day. If you plan on exercising in the morning and something comes up to throw off your schedule, what is the first thing you cross off your "to do" list? If you said exercise, you are not alone. It seems that for much of the population, exercise is low on the priority list. Take a minute to read Table 3-1 on the benefits of exercise. Although the table does not list every benefit of regular exercise, it may be enough to make you change your mind about beginning a regular exercise program.

The Centers for Disease Control and Prevention recommends light to moderate physical activity, preferably daily, for at least 30 minutes (1999), and the American Heart Association has stated that as little as 20 minutes of low-intensity exercise done three times per week is enough to see some cardiovascular benefit (1995). What, then, is the recommended amount of exercise for you? As you read further, you will see that an exercise program should be created for each individual according to his or her health history, personal goals, and schedule.

◆ *What does being active mean?*

It could start with simple changes within your workday. For example, Bill is a line foreman for an airline and has 13 airplane mechanics working for

TABLE 3-1. Benefits of Exercise

Benefits of Exercise

Prevent and manage cardiovascular disease
- Prevent plaque build-up in the arteries
- Improve circulation
- Reduce blood clot formation
- Control blood pressure
- Help manage angina and claudication

Improve breathing and oxygen use
- Decrease shortness of breath
- Deliver more oxygen to the heart and muscles

Strengthen muscles
- Make daily activities easier
- Strengthen the heart muscle
- Improve flexibility, balance, and general coordination

Strengthen bones
- Increase bone density and strength
- Decrease chance of broken bones
- Help prevent osteoporosis

Decrease anxiety and depression
- Increase feelings of control
- Increase release of mood-enhancing endorphins, which may improve your mood
- Promote relaxation and sleep

Decrease fats in the blood and body
- Improve appetite control and weight
- Decrease overall body fat
- Help control lipid levels

Boost immune system
- Promote the healing process
- Strengthen ability to recover from illness
- Increase resistance to illness

him. Their job is to fix the planes that need repairs. When he went back to work after his heart surgery, he admits that he was not treated much differently. He says, "You get around a bunch of mechanics like that, and they are not going to baby you a lot." He does admit that his co-workers would not let him carry things when he first came back to work. "A lot of times I would grab something like a coffeepot and they wouldn't let me do that [in the beginning]. Now they will let me," he says as he smiles. His employees also try to get Bill to be more healthy while on the job. "They say don't get on that golf cart—you need to walk down there. Now I find myself doing that. If I have time, I will walk."

—*Bill Day, open heart surgery survivor*

Part 3

Steps To Take Before Beginning an Exercise Program

When you decide you want to begin an exercise program, it is always good to talk to your doctor. To be truly effective, an activity program should be individualized for a person's goals and physical abilities. Just because your neighbor jogs two miles each day does not mean that type of workout is beneficial for you.

You may want to ask your doctor these questions before starting an exercise program:

- Given my personal health history, is there anything I need to be aware of before beginning an exercise program?
- Will any of my medications affect me when I am exercising? If so, how will they affect me, and what do I need to be aware of?
- What should my heart rate be when I am exercising? Will this target number ever change?
- How many times per week would you recommend I begin with? How many times per week should I work up to?

As you read through the rest of this chapter, realize that these recommendations are general guidelines for exercise and activity. Your health history is unique to you and may require special considerations that only you and your doctor are aware of. Again, please talk to your doctor before beginning an exercise program.

◆ *What is an exercise stress test?*

When you talk to your doctor about beginning an exercise program, you may be asked to take a stress test. This test will provide information about your cardiovascular system's response to exercise. However, an exercise stress test is not always needed before beginning an exercise program.

There are several variations of the exercise stress test. A general exercise stress test involves placing electrodes on your chest in order to get your electrocardiogram (EKG) reading. Then you will be asked to walk on a treadmill or ride on a stationary bicycle, which will increase in speed and elevation every two or three minutes until you tell the doctor and other health care professionals that you cannot walk or ride any longer. At that point, the test will be stopped. There may be times when your doctor will stop the test before you state that you are ready.

Variations of the exercise stress test include an EKG reading and the following:

- VO$_2$ max stress test: Breathing into a device that will test your gas exchange (for example, oxygen and carbon dioxide)
- Stress echocardiogram: Combining the exercise stress test with an echocardiogram
- Thallium stress test and Sestamibi stress test: Involving injection of an agent into your body to see a more advanced image of your heart

Part 4

Four Components of Fitness

Those who are considered fit can be described as "physically sound" or "healthy" (Berube, 1985). In addition, fitness is a measure of overall physical health which can be described in four components:

- Cardiovascular and pulmonary fitness
- Flexibility
- Muscular endurance
- Muscular strength

Each of these components is equally important for overall health and fitness. For example, if Joe is able to walk two miles each day but has trouble bending over to tie his shoes, he probably needs to work on his flexibility. If Mary has the flexibility to squat down and get into position to lift her ten-pound grandson but cannot actually lift him, she may need work on her muscular strength. The following paragraphs will describe the four components of fitness. As you read through this section, think about which components you may need to work on.

Cardiovascular and Pulmonary Fitness

When people refer to exercise, they often think only of the cardiovascular component. However, our pulmonary system is too important to be overlooked. Examples of activities that benefit the cardiovascular and pulmonary component of fitness include walking, jogging, swimming, bicycling, and aerobic dance. During these activities your heart, vessels, and lungs work together to deliver oxygen to your body. Your cardiovascular and pulmonary system will benefit from low- to moderate-intensity exercise; however, if you want to increase your fitness level it is important to exercise in your target heart rate zone (target heart rate is described later in this chapter).

Flexibility

Flexibility is being able to bend and move freely. The range of motion of a joint or the ability to move the joint freely involves flexibility of the muscles, tendons, and ligaments. Flexibility can be improved by stretching regularly four to five times each week. It is a good idea to perform stretches before and after cardiovascular exercise. Good flexibility makes daily living activities such as bending down to pick things up, getting in and out of a car, and stretching to reach for something over your head much easier.

Muscular Endurance★

Muscular endurance is the ability to lift light loads over and over again. Examples include sit-ups, push-ups, waxing a car, unloading dishes from the dishwasher and into the cabinet, making a bed, trimming hedges, and taking clothes from the dryer. You can train your muscles to have more endurance by using light hand weights and lifting them 15 to 20 times, 3 to 4 times per week. If you don't have hand weights, you can use household items such as an unopened can of soup. Remember to start out with small, light weights so you do not injure your muscles. Check with your doctor to see what type of muscular endurance exercise is best for you.

Muscular Strength★

Muscular strength is the ability to lift a heavy load one time. Examples of this include picking up grandkids, furniture, or filled trash bags, and getting out of chairs and bathtubs. You can strengthen your muscles by lifting heavier weights 6 to 10 times, 3 to 4 times per week.

Part 5

Creating an Exercise Program

You may be thinking that in order to achieve all of your goals you will need to exercise several hours at a time. As you read on, however, you will see that long periods of exercise each day are not necessary to achieve many health goals. There are four parts to any exercise program: mode, frequency, intensity, and duration. The following paragraphs will discuss these four parts in detail.

Mode

◆ *What is mode of exercise?*

Mode can be defined as "manner, way, or method of doing or acting" (Berube, 1985). Therefore, in the context of exercise, the word *mode* refers to what type of exercise you choose to do. It is important to note that

---

★If you begin a weightlifting program without understanding the proper way to lift, you may end up getting hurt. Just as with any other form of exercise, it is a good idea to check with your doctor to make sure that muscular strength and endurance exercises are safe for you. In addition, if you are exercising at a workout facility, be sure to have someone show you how to use the equipment properly to reduce your chances of getting hurt. If you are exercising at home, a number of books are specifically designed to show you how to do proper weightlifting exercises. Please lift weights knowledgeably and safely.

mode of exercise is an individual choice: what is great fun for one person may be agony for another.

◆ *What mode of exercise should I pick?*

There is no single mode of exercise that is correct for every person. It is very important that you choose an exercise that is enjoyable and comfortable for you. If you absolutely dislike cycling due to the discomfort of the bicycle seat, then pick a different exercise. For some people, the ideal mode of exercise changes from week to week or even from day to day. Many exercisers get bored doing the same type of exercise repeatedly and need a frequent change in order to keep going. It is not necessary to do the same exercise day after day and week after week for it to be effective. Remember that cardiovascular and pulmonary exercise is best for your heart, while a combination of cardiovascular, pulmonary, and strength-training exercise improves overall fitness.

◆ *What are different modes of exercise?*

There are many modes of exercise. The following lists have examples categorized by the component of fitness and, although not comprehensive, will give you several ideas.

Examples of cardiovascular and pulmonary exercise:

- Walking
- Hiking
- Jogging
- Cycling
- Skating
- Dancing
- Stair step machine
- Swimming
- Water aerobics
- Cross-country snow skiing

Examples of activities to improve muscular endurance, strength, and flexibility:

- Baseball/softball
- Weight-lifting/carrying heavy weights
- Calisthenics (sit-ups, push-ups)
- Hitting golf balls
- Racket sports
- Gymnastics

◆ *Are unstructured activities beneficial?*

Reflect for a moment on your childhood. Did you have endless energy back then? Were some of your favorite activities riding your bike, running around with the other neighborhood kids, climbing trees, roller-skating, walking the dog, swimming, skateboarding, or building forts in the backyard? Did you think of these things as exercise or were they just fun things to do?

An interesting thing happens as we transition from childhood to adulthood—exercise becomes a bad word. It is no longer about having fun instead, it is about regular, structured, and boring exercise. With several modes of exercise to choose from, adults can find activities that are fun and easy to do. Exercise does not have to be structured, such as playing a sport or riding a stationary bicycle in order to benefit your cardiovascular system. For example, if you enjoy dancing and gardening, you may be surprised to learn that dancing is a cardiovascular exercise and gardening is good for muscular strength, endurance, and flexibility.

Examples of beneficial daily activities include:

- Washing the car for 45 to 60 minutes
- Raking leaves for 30 minutes
- Climbing stairs for 15 minutes
- Washing windows/floors for 45 to 60 minutes
- Gardening for 30 to 45 minutes
- Wheeling yourself in a wheelchair for 30 to 40 minutes

Source: National Heart, Lung, and Blood Institute, 2000

Frequency

Frequency of exercise refers to how many days per week you exercise. Just as mode of exercise is an individual choice, so is frequency of exercise. When determining how many days per week you want to exercise, you will first want to determine why you are choosing to exercise. Table 3-2

TABLE 3-2. Frequency of Exercise Based on Goals

My goal is to	I should exercise
Strengthen my heart and muscles	3 to 4 days a week (Rest 1 or 2 days between workouts.)
Help my heart, strengthen muscles, and also control diabetes, vascular pain, weight, and depression	6 or 7 days a week (Do a lighter workout or change your activity 1 or 2 days a week.)

might help you pick how many days per week you want to exercise based on your goal for being active.

As you can see, the ideal number of days per week of exercise varies for each person and depends on personal goals. Table 3-3 lists guidelines of three leading health authorities.

Many people might ask, "What is the minimum amount that I need to exercise in order to help my heart?" The answer to this question is three to four days per week, according to the American Heart Association. However, as you can see from Table 3-3, the ideal frequency of exercise is "most days of the week" in order to gain overall health benefits.

TABLE 3-3. Guidelines for Activity

Organization	Website	Activity Guideline
American Heart Association	www.americanheart.org	Regular, moderate-intensity physical activity 30 minutes or longer on most days
Centers for Disease Control and Prevention	www.cdc.gov	Regular, preferably daily, light to moderate physical activity for at least 30 minutes
National Heart, Lung, and Blood Institute	www.nhlbi.nih.gov	At least 30 minutes of moderate-intensity physical activity on most, and preferably all, days of the week

◆ *Can I over exercise?*

Exercising too hard every day can lead to what is called over-use syndrome. This syndrome can result in injury, fatigue, and boredom and can be a result of over exercising. Just as your body needs sleep as a form of rest, it also needs rest from exercise. It is a balancing act between how much exercise is enough and when it becomes too much. If you are exercising seven days per week and find yourself tired much of the time or if you are getting injured frequently, it may be time to take a break from exercising for a few days and check with your doctor to determine if you are over exercising.

A second form of exercising too much is called the "weekend warrior syndrome." Have you ever met anyone who gets no exercise during the week but on the weekends runs, cycles, swims, and plays in the company softball game? This is a classic example of a weekend warrior. Not exercising regularly and then working very hard for one or two days in a row can lead to injury and is stressful on the heart and other muscles.

Intensity

When you are exercising it is beneficial to know how hard you need to be working. In other words, you need to know what "intensity" to strive for. How do you know when you are working out too hard? How do you know when you are not working out hard enough? Adjusting your exercise intensity is a balancing act, just as adjusting your exercise frequency is.

There are several ways to determine what exercise intensity is ideal for you. The methods discussed in this book are:

- Target heart rate
- Talk vs. sing rule
- Rating of perceived exertion

Target Heart Rate

Your target heart rate is what your heart rate should be when you are exercising. Refer to Chapter 1 to learn about your resting heart rate and

TABLE 3-4. Sample Calculations of Maximum and Target Heart Rate

Shaun's maximum heart rate:	220	Constant number that is used for all ages
	- 52	Shaun's age in years
	168	Shaun's predicted maximum heart rate
Shaun's target heart rate:	168	Shaun's predicted maximum heart rate
	×.70	70%
	118	The low end of Shaun's target heart rate
	168	Shaun's predicted maximum heart rate
	×.85	85%
	143	The high end of Shaun's target heart rate

In this example, since Shaun is 52 years old, her target heart rate range for exercise is 118 to 143 beats per minute.

Source: Franklin, 2000

how to take your heart rate. Your target heart rate can be calculated using values obtained from an exercise test or by established formulas. Your doctor or a health professional can help determine your target heart rate. An exercise stress test is the most accurate way to determine your target heart rate. Mathematical formulas can also be used.

The *American College of Sports Medicine Guidelines for Exercise Testing and Prescription* (Sixth Edition) describes the "percentage of heart rate maximum" as one way to calculate your target heart rate range. In this formula, 70% to 85% of your maximum heart rate is your heart rate range. Your maximum heart rate is determined by taking 220 minus your age. An example of this formula appears in Table 3-4.

It is important to note that the formula in Table 3-4 is for persons who are apparently healthy and have no symptoms of cardiovascular disease. However, even if you are relatively young and think you do not have cardiovascular disease, you may want to discuss this formula with your doctor before beginning an exercise program.

If you have cardiovascular disease, many popular methods for calculating target heart rate may not apply to you. For instance, a class of medications called beta-blockers will control and slow down your heart rate. This is normal if you are on a beta-blocker, so your target heart rate range will need to be adjusted.

Talk vs. Sing Rule

There are methods to determine your intensity level other than taking your heart rate. The talk vs. sing rule for determining exercise intensity is perhaps the easiest to use. The guideline is relatively simple:

- When exercising you should be able to talk comfortably back and forth with your workout partner.
- If you are working out so hard that you do not have enough breath to speak, this is a signal that you are working too hard and you need to slow down your pace.

Keep in mind that talking should be somewhat more difficult when you are exercising than it normally is, but you should still be able to carry on a conversation. On the other hand, if you are able to sing while exercising, you are most likely not getting a good workout and you need to increase your intensity. Although the talk vs. sing rule sounds simplistic, it is something that each person can use to determine his or her proper intensity level. This method is truly about listening to your body and how it is reacting to exercise.

Rating of Perceived Exertion (RPE) Scale

The Rating of Perceived Exertion (RPE) scale was created by Gunnar Borg, Ph.D., and is a reliable way to determine your exercise intensity. You may have seen the RPE scale in your doctor's office if you have had an exercise stress test. The scale was developed to allow a person who is exercising to rate his or her feelings during exercise. Dr. Borg has created two scales: the original RPE scale (Table 3.5), which goes from 6 to 20, and the category-ratio scale (Table 3.6), which goes from 0 to 10. The RPE scale can provide many exercisers with an easily understood guideline for exercise intensity.

Duration

Duration of exercise means how long you should exercise. This is an individual choice depending on your current level of fitness as well as your personal goals. Refer to Table 3-7 to determine how long to exercise according to your personal goals.

TABLE 3-5. The Original RPE Scale

While exercising, rate your perception of exertion; i.e., how heavy and strenuous the exercise feels to you. The perception of exertion depends mainly on the strain and fatigue in your muscles and on your feeling of breathlessness or aches in the chest. Look at this rating scale; use this scale from 6–20, where 6 means "no exertion at all" and 20 means "maximal exertion."

6	No exertion at all	13	Somewhat hard
7		14	
8	Extremely light	15	Hard (heavy)
		16	
9		17	Very hard
10		18	
11	Light	19	Extremely hard
12		20	Maximal exertion

9 corresponds to "very light" exercise. For a normal, healthy person it is like walking slowly at his or her own pace for some minutes.

13 on the scale is "somewhat hard" exercise, but it still feels OK to continue.

17 "very hard" is very strenuous. A healthy person can still go on, but he or she really has to push him or herself. It feels very heavy and the person is very tired.

19 on the scale is an extremely strenuous exercise level. For most people this is the most strenuous exercise they have ever experienced.

Try to appraise your feeling of exertion as honestly as possible, without thinking about what the actual physical load is. Don't underestimate it, but don't overestimate it either. It's your own feeling of effort and exertion that's important, not how it compares to other people's. What other people think is not important either. Look at the scale and the expressions and give a number.

TABLE 3-6. Category Ratio (CR-10) Scale

0	Nothing at All	No "I"
0.3		
0.5	Extremely weak	Just noticeable
0.7		
1	Very weak	
1.5		
2	Weak	Light easy
2.5		
3	Moderate	
4		
5	Strong	Heavy difficult
6		
7	Very strong	
8		
9		
10	Extremely strong	Strongest "I"
11		
• Absolute maximum		Highest possible
		Note: "I" stands for intensity.

Copyright Gunnar Borg, 1982, 1998. Reprinted with permission. For correct usage of the CR-10 scale it is necessary to follow the information about scaling, additional administration, and instruction, which can be obtained together with separate scales directly from Gunnar Borg, Borg Perception, Furuholmen 1027, 76291 Rimbo Sweden.

TABLE 3-7. Duration of Exercise Based on Goals

Personal Fitness Goal	Exercise Duration
Improve my cardiovascular fitness	15 to 30 minutes
Lose weight	45 to 60 minutes (at a low intensity)

Note: This time does not include your warm up and cool down.

◆ *What if I am unable to exercise for the full duration?*

If you cannot exercise for the full duration, exercise in short intervals. For example, walk briskly for 5 minutes, rest 2 minutes, and then begin walking again. Keep repeating these intervals until you have exercised a total of

15 minutes. As your fitness level improves, increase your exercise time and decrease your rest periods. An important tip to remember is that you want to increase your duration before your intensity. In other words, try going longer and longer until you reach your time goal and only then increase the level of difficulty. It is better to walk slowly for 15 to 20 minutes than to walk fast but only be able to last 3 to 5 minutes. Remember to use the target heart rate, rating of perceived exertion or talk vs. sing methods as you increase intensity, so that you do not over exercise.

◆ *What if I want to exercise for 30 minutes but my schedule will not allow me to?*

If your schedule does not allow for 30 minutes of exercise, you can split your exercise into different time segments. For example, try exercising 15 minutes before and after work or 10 minutes before work, during lunch, and after work. If your only goal is to reduce your risk of cardiovascular disease, then this type of exercise will be beneficial to you. If, however, you wish to lose weight, you will probably need to exercise for the more traditional longer periods of time. Even if you are trying to lose weight, splitting your exercise time into segments is better than no exercise at all.

Part 6
Other Things to Consider

◆ *What time of day is best to exercise?*

The best time of day to exercise is the time that works for you. If you are a morning person, you may choose to exercise when you first wake up. On the other hand, if you are a night owl who likes staying up late, the evening may work better for you. If you exercise in the evening remember that the later you work out, the more difficult it may be to fall asleep. Depending on what you do, your exercise routine may have to be worked around your schedule. Try to pick a time of day that you can commit to, rather than choosing a time that you know probably will not work. Also, it is acceptable to rotate your exercise time to the mornings on some days and the afternoons or evenings on others.

The main tip to remember when deciding when to exercise is to wait two to three hours after a large meal. Use common sense with this tip; if you have just had an apple, that does not make up a "large meal" and, therefore, there is no need to wait several hours before you exercise. In contrast, if you just finished a holiday feast, you may need to extend the waiting time to three or four hours.

◆ *How do I warm up and cool down?*

The warm-up and cool-down are very important. Warming up means moving your muscles and doing proper stretches before starting your exercise. This can reduce injury from tight muscles and increase your heart rate gradually. After your warm-up, stretch all your major muscle groups. Here are a few tips to follow when stretching:

- Exercise at a lower intensity for 5 to 10 minutes.
- Stretch only to the point at which you feel tightness in your muscles, not pain.
- Do not bounce when stretching.
- Hold each stretch for 15 to 30 seconds.

It is important to perform proper stretching exercises. Improper stretching can lead to injury and discomfort. Many of the "old ways" of stretching, such as bouncing, have been determined unsafe and can put a strain on your back. Please consult with an exercise specialist for proper stretching techniques.

Cooling down means gradually reducing your intensity before you stop the exercise. After each exercise session, allow five to ten minutes to cool down by doing lower-intensity exercise. For example, slow down your pace for the last five to ten minutes of exercise. Doing this allows your heart rate and breathing to slow down gradually. Stopping exercise suddenly may result in dizziness and sometimes fainting. You may also want to stretch again after your exercise session. At this point, your muscles are warm and stretching might be easier. Stretching before and after exercise is a great habit to establish for overall fitness.

◈ *What should I wear when I exercise?*

What you wear during exercise is important for your comfort and safety. Here are some quick tips for wearing appropriate clothing:

- Wear loose-fitting, light-colored, cotton clothing.
- Wear properly fitted shoes.
- If your doctor has recommended that you wear TED™ stockings or support hose, wear cotton socks over them.

You do not have to buy new clothes for exercising. Many people have casual clothing that is appropriate for activity. However, one thing you may consider buying is a new pair of shoes. If your tennis shoes are more than one year old, it is time to buy a new pair. You need to exercise in shoes that are designed for activity, such as tennis shoes or sneakers. Boots, sandals, and even some lace-up style tennis shoes are stylish and good for daily wear but are not appropriate for exercising. A good pair of workout shoes does not necessarily mean the most expensive pair. Last year's model will probably work great and will cost you half as much as the newer model.

Look for shoes that give you proper support, and realize that many athletic shoe specialty stores have personnel trained to assist you in finding the appropriate shoes. Proper footwear is very important because of the strain on your feet, lower extremities, and back during exercise and activity. You may have guessed that wearing old, run-down, or improperly fitting shoes may lead to muscle injury and blisters. But did you know that it can also lead to back soreness and pain? Here are some tips on purchasing new shoes:

- Choose a store that has knowledgeable salespeople.
- Try on several brands and styles until you find a comfortable pair.
- Buy shoes in the afternoon or evening since your feet may expand throughout the day.
- Walk around in the store to test the shoes for comfort and proper fit.

- Choose a shoe with a close-fitting heel and proper arch support.
- Allow a thumb's width of space between your toes and the front of the shoe.
- Replace your shoes every six months if you wear them for everyday activity and exercising.

◆ *What do I need to consider in hot weather?*

It is difficult for your body to cool down when you exercise in the heat. To help prevent any heat-related emergencies, follow these tips when you are exercising in hot weather:

- Decrease your exercise intensity.
- Pay close attention to your Rating of Perceived Exertion and heart rate.
- Avoid the hottest parts of the day, usually between 11:00 a.m. and 5:00 p.m.
- Drink water before, during, and after your exercise session. Do not take salt tablets.
- Use sunblock and wear a hat.
- Be aware that if you are taking a beta-blocker, your body's ability to maintain a constant temperature is affected, and your risk of getting overheated may be increased.
- Avoid outdoor exercise when temperatures and humidity are high. See Table 3-8 for the heat index chart.
- Never wear rubber suits or sweat suits in an effort to lose weight. This may cause serious health risks as your body can overheat quickly.

Heat Index Chart

The heat index indicates the temperature that your body feels, not the air temperature that a thermometer measures. The relative humidity combines with the air temperature to create the heat index. You have probably heard your local weather person state the "relative humidity" for the day in your city. If you know the humidity level and the temperature, you can determine the heat index by looking at Table 3-8. In Table 3-8, the first column on the left is the relative humidity and the top line is the air temperature. The heat index values can be read as follows:

- Any value less than 80 is considered comfortable.
- Any value greater than 90 is considered extreme.
- Any value greater than 100 is considered hazardous.
- Any value greater than 110 is considered dangerous.

Table 3-8. Heat Index Table★

Humidity								
100%	72	80	91	108				
95%	71	79	89	105				
90%	71	79	88	102	122			
85%	71	78	87	99	117			
80%	71	78	86	97	113	136		
75%	70	77	86	95	109	130		
70%	70	77	85	93	106	124	144	
65%	70	76	83	91	102	119	138	
60%	70	76	82	90	100	114	132	149
55%	69	75	81	89	98	110	126	142
50%	69	75	81	88	96	107	120	135
45%	68	74	80	87	95	104	115	129
40%	68	74	79	86	93	101	110	123
35%	67	73	79	85	91	98	107	118
30%	67	73	78	84	90	96	104	113
25%	66	72	77	83	88	94	101	109
20%	66	72	77	82	87	93	99	105
15%	65	71	76	81	86	91	97	102
10%	65	70	75	80	85	90	95	100
5%	64	69	74	79	84	88	93	97
0%	64	69	73	78	83	87	91	95
	70	75	80	85	90	95	100	105
	Air Temperature (°F)							

★Formulas taken from the National Weather Service Office in Newport, North Carolina.

Use great caution when exercising outdoors if the heat index is in the "extreme" category. When it is in the "hazardous" or "dangerous" range, it is a good idea to find indoor alternatives such as mall walking, swimming, dancing, or going to your local fitness club. Remember from Chapter 2 that some medications prevent your body from cooling down normally and others make your skin more sensitive to sunlight, so check with your doctor or pharmacist to see if you need to take special precautions.

◆ *What about exercising in cold weather?*

Exercising in cold weather can also put added strain on your body because the body must use extra energy to keep warm. Refer to Table 3-9 for the wind chill chart. Here are a few tips to remember if you choose to exercise in cold weather:

- Avoid outdoor exercise when temperatures and/or the wind chill factor are unusually low. Check with your doctor to see what temperature is recommended for you.
- Stay dry. If your clothes get wet they will not insulate you from the cold.
- Wear several light layers of clothes including a hat and gloves. As you warm up during your exercise session, you may want to remove some layers of clothing. If you wear one thick layer, you might get too warm.

◆ *What do I need to know about air pollution?*

Air pollution can be more than just a nuisance when exercising outdoors. Here are a few tips to consider if you plan to exercise outdoors:

TABLE 3-9. Wind Chill Chart*.

Temp. (°F)	Wind Chill Factor						
-25	-31	-52	-65	-74	-81	-86	-89
-20	-26	-46	-58	-67	-74	-79	-82
-15	-21	-40	-51	-60	-66	-71	-74
-10	-15	-34	-45	-51	-59	-64	-67
-5	-10	-27	-38	-46	-51	-59	-64
0	-5	-22	-31	-39	-44	-49	-52
5	0	-15	-25	-31	-36	-41	-43
10	6	-9	-18	-24	-29	-33	-35
15	11	-3	-11	-17	-22	-25	-27
20	16	3	-5	-10	-15	-18	-20
25	22	10	2	-3	-7	-10	-12
30	27	16	9	4	1	-2	-4
35	32	22	16	12	8	6	4
40	37	28	23	19	16	13	12
45	43	34	29	26	23	21	20
	5	10	15	20	25	30	35
	Wind Speed (mph)						

*Formulas taken from weatherpoint.com.

- Be aware of ozone alert/warning days. Exposure to pollutants in the atmosphere can cause inflammation in the respiratory system, especially for persons with lung disease. This exposure is less of a problem in the early mornings and late evenings.
- Avoid walking or jogging along busy streets to decrease your exposure to pollutants.

◆ What should I consider when in high altitudes?

- There are fewer oxygen molecules in the air at higher altitudes. It may be harder for you to breathe and, therefore, harder to exercise. Talk with your doctor if you are planning on exercising when taking a trip to a city that is at an altitude you are not used to.
- Also, adjust your exercise intensity to keep your Rating of Perceived Exertion and heart rate within normal ranges.

◆ What can I do to help avoid injuries when exercising?

If you have been inactive, exercise can lead to injuries when proper care is not used. It is important to begin at a slow pace and increase your intensity gradually as you become fit. Once you become fit, you will notice that your muscles are stronger and you will be less likely to suffer injuries. Following are a few tips to avoid injuries due to exercise.

Blisters

- Prevent blisters by wearing appropriate shoes and socks. Proper foot care is especially important for people with diabetes and peripheral vascular disease.

Muscle Aches, Cramps, and Strains

- Warm up and stretch properly.
- Increase your exercise gradually over time.
- If you have an injury, choose a type of exercise that does not use the injured area until it heals.

Joint Sprains

- Exercise in a lighted environment on level ground.
- Wear properly fitted shoes.

◆ Do I need to avoid sexual activity if I am a heart patient?

You may want to talk with your doctor regarding sexual activity; the general guideline is that you can resume sexual activity as soon as you feel you are ready. Sexual activity can lead to a rapid heart rate, faster breathing, and flushed skin. This is normal and not a sign of strain on your heart. The following are some helpful tips regarding sexual activity:

- Depression, changes in mood, and/or heart medication may affect sexual activity. If you have concerns, talk to your doctor.
- Choose a time when you are rested, relaxed, and free from stressful feelings.
- Select a familiar, peaceful setting that is free of interruptions.
- For patients with recent open-heart surgery, avoid positions that may increase strain to your breastbone until it is completely healed (for example, holding yourself up with your arms). The healing process for your breastbone takes approximately six to eight weeks.

◆ Can I perform household activities if I am a heart patient?

The guidelines for sexual activity also apply for household activities. Activities such as washing the car, cleaning, lifting light items, taking out the trash, and vacuuming can be resumed when you feel ready. If you recently had open-heart surgery, check with your doctor before lifting anything over 10 pounds.

◆ Are there other medical considerations regarding exercise?

Establishing a regular routine of exercise and activity is important to living a healthy life. However, there are situations when exercising should be closely evaluated. Following are a few conditions to consider:

Illness

If you are sick (for example, fever, cold, or flu), you should not exercise. Your body is already working hard to get you well and does not need the added stress of exercise. When you recover, start back at a lower intensity and gradually return to your usual level of activity. The general guideline is to exercise two days at a lighter intensity for every one day that you were sick. For example, if you were sick for three days, when you are feeling better exercise at a lighter intensity for the six days following your illness.

Diabetes

- Talk with your doctor or diabetes specialist before beginning any exercise program.
- Monitor your blood sugar before and after exercise. If your blood sugar is consistently over 250 mg/dL, consult your doctor before exercising.

- If you take insulin, inject it into a muscle that will not be very active during your workout (for example, your stomach muscles).
- Avoid exercising during peak hours of your insulin activity.
- Have a carbohydrate snack readily available.
- Exercise with a workout partner who is familiar with your diabetes.
- Wear some form of medical identification to alert people to the fact that you have diabetes.
- Talk to your doctor about the need to adjust your insulin dose and/or diet due to your increased exercise activity.

Peripheral Vascular Disease (PVD)

- If you have peripheral vascular disease, walk until you can no longer tolerate the claudication pain. Rest until the pain subsides and then begin walking again. Repeat this process until your goal for exercise time is met.

Chest Pain

- If you are having chest pain, do not exercise without your doctor's approval.

Conclusion

Now that you know about many of the benefits of regular activity and you have read about how to exercise properly, you are on your way to living an active and healthy life. Remember that there will be challenges ahead, and some days you may not feel like exercising. The key to sticking with any exercise program is to establish a habit. Making exercise a part of your daily routine becomes easier once the habit is established. The rewards of an active lifestyle such as feeling stronger, having more energy, having less body aches and pains, and possibly shedding excess weight may motivate you to continue exercising. Exercise also has a positive impact on cardiovascular risk factors such as blood pressure, cholesterol level, body fat and body weight, and diabetes. Exercise also may help to control tobacco use.

The ultimate reward is feeling good about yourself and your health. This peace of mind can affect other aspects of your life and improve your overall mental well-being.

4

Nutrition and Healthful Eating

> "Have you ever seen the tubes with the fat in it? Those were impressive. I really thought I would like to have some like that to show somebody. I haven't had a doughnut, I gave up eggs, I haven't had any prime rib, and, boy, that was tough. I have really changed my whole way of living. And my wife has too. She made some cholesterol-free, fat-free minestrone soup that was delicious. I like meat and I still eat meat, but I do it like they tell me: no bigger than a deck of cards. At Christmas and Thanksgiving I ate, and I ate pretty much what I wanted to, but I stayed away from the sweet bar, you know the dessert trays and all. And I think I gained one pound between the two holidays, but I got rid of that going to exercise."
>
> *Bill Day, Open Heart Surgery Survivor*

The following A-B-C guidelines were developed to help you and your family enjoy sensible and nourishing food while taking action for optimal health. Each guideline will be discussed individually to help fit your lifestyle and possibly prevent or slow the development of cardiovascular disease.

Aim for fitness:

- Aim for a healthful weight.
- Be physically active each day.

Build a healthful base:
- Let the pyramid guide your food choices.
- Choose a variety of grains daily, especially whole grains.
- Choose a variety of fruits and vegetables daily.

Choose sensibly:
- Choose a diet that is low in saturated fat and cholesterol and moderate in total fat.
- Choose beverages and foods that limit your intake of sugars.
- Choose and prepare foods with less salt.
- If you drink alcoholic beverages, do so in moderation.

Part I
Aim for Fitness

A Healthful Weight

In order to stay at or reach a healthful body weight, good eating habits and regular physical activity need to be a part of your plan. Do you know what your "healthful weight" is? A variety of methods are used to determine a healthful weight. Table 4-1 is a body mass index (BMI) chart; consulting it is one way to find out if your weight is appropriate for your height. However, BMI is only a guide; the weight that is best for you depends on many things, including your gender, height, age, and heredity. Talk to your doctor and/or registered dietitian about what body weight is healthful for your age and medical history.

Physical Activity

For more information on how to become more physically active, see Chapter 3, Active Living.

Part 2
Build a Healthful Base

A Balanced Meal

Figure 4-1 shows what comprises a balanced meal. Two-thirds of the meal is based on grains (especially whole grains), vegetables, and fruits; and one-third of the meal is from protein-rich sources (low-fat milk, yogurt, and cheese; lean meats, poultry, and fish; beans, nuts, and soy).

TABLE 4-1 Body Mass Index (BMI) Chart

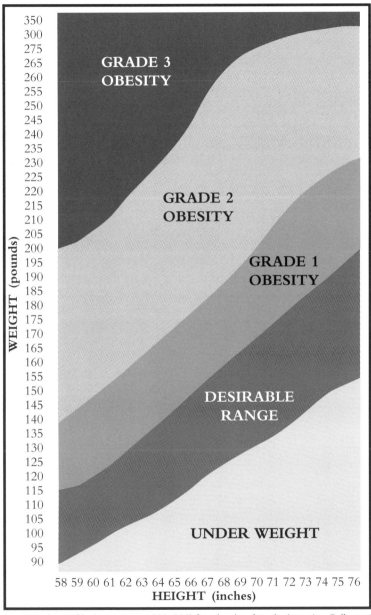

Source: Baylor Health Care Systems, 1998. BMI formula taken from the Amercian College of Sports Medicine Guidelines, 1997.

FIGURE 4-1. A Balanced Meal

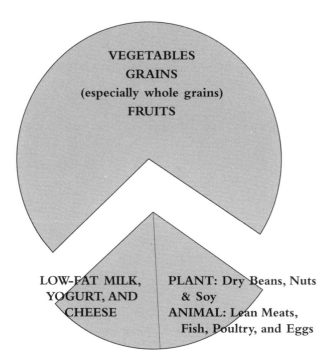

Dietary fat is often associated with a combination of carbohydrates and protein-rich foods, with more fat found in protein-rich foods. The key is to let fat occur naturally in your diet, rather than as an added source. Moreover, the basis of fat intake should come from unsaturated rather than saturated fat sources.

This is only a guideline to assist you with your journey to optimal nourishment. It is up to you to discover and explore the best way to nourish your body. Learning to work with your body, not against it, will enable you to achieve ultimate success—good health.

Nutrition is exciting. There are many ways to provide your body with the "building blocks" or nourishment it needs to function at its best. Apply the basic guidelines described in this chapter, and find out for yourself the enormous benefits of eating sensibly.

The Food Guide Pyramid

Your body needs a variety of nutrients each day to function at its best. Different foods and food groups consist of different nutrients as well as other healthful substances (only found in food). No individual food or food group can provide all the nutrients you need; therefore, eating a variety of foods is essential for good health. Eating a variety means providing your body with different nutrients, vitamins and minerals, flavors, textures, and colors that make food pleasurable.

Use the Food Guide Pyramid in Figure 4-2 as a guide to shape your eating patterns. The Food Guide Pyramid can help balance your food

FIGURE 4-2. The Food Guide Pyramid

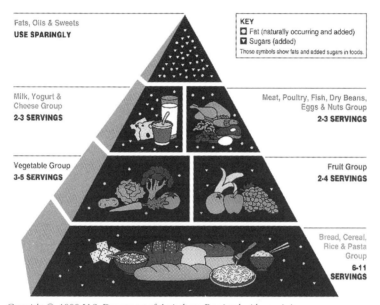

Copyright © 1999 U.S. Department of Agriculture. Reprinted with permission.

choices. Let plant foods such as whole grains, vegetables, and fruits be the center of your meals or the foundation of your pyramid. Eat moderate amounts of foods rich in protein such as lean meat, fish and poultry, eggs, beans, and nuts, as well as low-fat milk, yogurt, and cheese. Sparingly use added fats, oils, sweets, and sugars.

◆ What is a serving size?

Serving sizes are a guide to assist you in meeting your daily nutrient needs. Use Figure 4-2 to determine how much of each food you are getting each day. Is your pyramid balanced?

The serving size examples in Table 4-2 are not to replace your body's signals of hunger and fullness. Listen to your body: eat when you are

TABLE 4-2. Examples of a Single Serving Size in Different Food Groups

Bread, cereal, rice, and pasta group 1 slice of bread 1 tortilla ½ cup cooked cereal ½ cup cooked rice or pasta ½ hamburger roll, bagel, pita or English muffin 3-4 crackers 1 pancake (4-inch) 1 cup dry cereal (flakes) *Meat, poultry (chicken), fish, dry beans, eggs, and nuts group* 3 ounces cooked lean beef, pork, lamb, veal, chicken, or fish ½ cup cooked beans 1 egg 2 t. peanut butter ½ cup nuts	*Vegetable group* ½ cup chopped raw or cooked vegetables *Milk, yogurt, and cheese group* 1 cup low-fat milk 1 cup low-fat yogurt 1½ ounces natural cheese *Fats, oils, and sweets* 1 tsp. oil (canola, olive, peanut, vegetable) 1 tsp. butter or margarine 1 tsp. regular mayonnaise 1 Tbsp. light mayonnaise 1 Tbsp. regular salad dressing 2 Tbsp. light salad dressing *Fruit group* 1 piece of fruit or melon wedge ¾ cup 100% fruit juice ¼ cup dried fruit ½ cup chopped, cooked, or canned fruit

hungry and finish eating when you are full. These are healthful skills that can help maintain your proper body weight; however, they take practice.

◆ *How many servings do I need each day?*

Table 4-3 will help you determine how many servings you need.

Grains, Fruits, and Vegetables

◆ *Why do I need whole grains, vegetables, and fruits?*

Whole grains, vegetables, and fruits are the base for healthful eating. They make up the foundation of the Food Guide Pyramid and are the center of a balanced meal. These plant foods are low in fat, unless fat is added

TABLE 4-3. The Number of Servings Needed

Food group	Women, some older adults (1,600 calories)	Active women, most men (2,200 calories)	Active men (2,800 calories)
Bread, rice, cereal, and grains (especially whole grains)	6	9	11
Vegetables	3	4	5
Fruits	2	3	4
Low-fat milk, yogurt, and cheese	2–3	2–3	2–3
Dry beans, eggs, nuts, fish, lean meat, and poultry	5 ounces	6 ounces	7 ounces

Adapted from United States Department of Agriculture, the Food Guide Pyramid.

during processing or preparation; they are a good source of carbohydrates, including dietary fiber (Table 4-4), and they provide a wealth of vitamins including antioxidants (Table 4-5), minerals, and useful phytochemicals (Table 4-6). The dietary guidelines recommend that you consume six or more servings of grains (Figure 4-3), especially whole grains, and five to nine servings of vegetables and fruits daily.

Quick & Easy Fiber Ideas

- Choose 100% whole-wheat bread (2–6 grams per slice).
- Serve fresh fruit for dessert (3–5 grams per cup).
- Keep raw vegetables on hand for snacking (4 grams per cup).
- Leave the peels on your fruits and potatoes (1–3 grams per serving).
- Try baked beans, chili, bean soup, bean salsa, or other bean dishes three or more times a week (5–8 grams per ½ cup).

FIGURE 4-3.

Hop Aboard the Grain Train

The first stop is good health.

❖ Recommendations for healthful eating advise us to base our meals on grains especially whole grains.

❖ The Food Guide Pyramid places all grains (both whole and refined) together, however, it is important to realize that not all grains are created equal.

WHOLE GRAINS	REFINED GRAINS
• Rich sources of dietary fiber (soluble and insoluble) • Loaded with nutrients such as iron, zinc, and B-vitamins • Contains a wealth of phytochemicals (useful plant compounds), which may be beneficial to your health	• Contains minimal to no dietary fiber, nutrients, and phytochemicals, because these important nutrients have been lost during processing (refining).

❖ The key to good health lies in choosing whole grains, not just refined grains. Refined grains may contain some fiber, but recent research suggests it's the whole food (including the vitamins, minerals, phytochemicals, etc.), not just the fiber, that possesses the disease-preventing health benefits.

❖ This doesn't mean that every morsel of grain eaten must be whole grain. Enjoy a variety of grains with emphasis placed on whole grains.

❖ Leading experts recommend that you consume three or more servings of whole grains per day.

❖ **What is a Whole Grain?**

Look for the following on ingredient labels to help you choose whole grains:

Whole barley	Cracked Wheat	Whole Rye
Bulgur	Whole Oats	Quinoa
Whole Cornmeal	Graham Flour	Millet
Flaxseed Meal	Whole Wheat	Brown Rice

❖ **Tips for adding more whole grains to your diet:**
- Add bulgur to salads and pilafs
- Enjoy oatmeal and other whole grain cereals for breakfast
- Add Quinoa or barley to soups and stews
- Mix ground flaxseed into breads or atop salads and casseroles
- Use a variety of whole grain breads to dress up your meals

TABLE 4-4. Sources, Functions and Recommended Servings of Fiber.

Sources of fiber*	**Insoluble:** Rye, wheat bran, whole grains, seeds, fruit and vegetable peels, soy. **Soluble:** Fruits, legumes, oats, vegetables, soy, nuts, and barley
Function of fiber	Fiber is found only in plants. It is a complex carbohydrate that is not digested by the body. Most of the benefits associated with fiber consumption appear to be related to the fact that it is not digestible. The presence of fiber in the diet may have considerable impact on many diseases, including cardiovascular disease. Dietary fiber promotes a healthy digestive tract. Research suggests that soluble fiber may help to reduce total blood cholesterol, as well as alter the lipid profile. Furthermore, soluble fiber may delay the transit of nutrients through the digestive tract and delay the absorption of blood sugar (helping with the management of blood sugars). Soluble fiber may also decrease blood pressure. Insoluble fiber aids with digestive functioning. Additionally, insoluble fiber may reduce the risk of gallstones, diverticulitis, colon cancer, and obesity.
Recommendations	Leading experts recommend that you consume 20 to 35 grams of dietary fiber daily. Eat a variety of fiber-rich sources, including both soluble and insoluble, for optimal health benefit.

*Increase the total fiber content of your diet slowly and drink eight to ten cups of water per day to help with hydration and nutrient transport. The increased water will help you avoid discomfort as you increase your fiber intake.

TABLE 4-5. Sources, Functions, and Recommended Servings of Antioxidants★

Nutrient	Sources	Function	Recommendations
Vitamin E	Polyunsaturated oils (corn, vegetable, sunflower, safflower, and soybean), leafy green vegetables, wheat germ, whole grain products, egg yolks, nuts, and seeds	May protect low-density lipoprotein and polyunsaturated fats against oxidation (destruction), reducing the risk of cardiovascular disease. May prevent blood clots and formation of fatty plaques.	100 to 400 IU/day★★
Vitamin C	Citrus, cabbage-type vegetables, dark green vegetables, cantaloupe, strawberries, peppers, tomatoes, potatoes, papayas, and mangos.	Enhances the resistance of low-density lipoprotein (LDL) to oxidation. May help to maintain blood vessel flexibility, resulting in blood pressure benefits.	Adequate intake is easily achieved by eating five to nine servings of vegetables and fruits per day.
Carotenoids (beta-carotene, lycopene, lutein, zeaxantin)	Dark green, deep orange, yellow, and red vegetables and fruits, including tomatoes, carrots, spinach, broccoli, sweet potatoes, and pumpkin	Thought to assist in the prevention of fat oxidation.	Aim for five to nine servings per day of a variety of colorful vegetables and fruits.

★It has been suggested that vitamins, minerals, antioxidants, and phytochemicals work best as a team, not as a single nutrient.
★★Talk to your doctor before taking a vitamin E supplement.

Table 4-6. Sources, Functions, and Recommended Servings of Phytochemicals*

Nutrient	Sources	Function	Recommendations
Flavonoids	Celery, cranberries, onions, kale, broccoli, apples, cherries, berries, green and black tea, wine, parsley, soybeans, tomatoes, eggplant, and thyme	May protect against damage done by cholesterol and help to prevent blood clots.	
Organosulfurs	Onions, garlic, leeks, chives, scallions, and shallots.	May have beneficial effects on cholesterol levels (may reduce a proportion of cholesterol in the liver).	Studies report that heating garlic may block its health effects; however, if crushed fresh garlic is allowed to stand 10 minutes before heating, it is thought that the beneficial chemicals are released and not lost when garlic is cooked and/or heated. Garlic supplements show little benefit.
Phytoestrogens (plant estrogens)	Soy protein, whole grains, berries, fruits, vegetables, and ground flax seed	Studies associate phytoestrogens with lower levels of total cholesterol, low-density lipoprotein (LDL), and triglycerides.	

**It has been suggested that vitamins, minerals, antioxidants, and phytochemicals work best as a team, not as single nutrients.*

Part 3

Choose Sensibly

Limiting Fat and Cholesterol

◆ *How much fat is sensible to eat?*

Leading experts recommend that less than 30% of your total calories come from fat. Fat is an essential nutrient; however, it is not the base of the nutrient intake, as illustrated by the Food Guide Pyramid. Grains (especially whole grains), vegetables, and fruits are the base and/or foundation of our nutrient needs.

Fat can be classified as saturated or unsaturated. There are two types of unsaturated fat: polyunsaturated and monounsaturated. Saturated fat is primarily found in animal foods, whereas unsaturated fat is primarily found in plants. It is recommended to replace the intake of saturated fat with unsaturated fat without increasing the total fat intake. Refer to Tables 4-7, 4-8, and 4-9 for sources, functions, and recommendations for eating saturated, polyunsaturated and monounsaturated fat.

Use the recommended calorie and fat levels in Table 4-10 to determine the recommended grams of total fat, saturated fat, and unsaturated fat for your calorie needs. Talk with your doctor or dietitian to determine how many calories you need each day.

> Fast occurs naturaly in anumber of foods. To include fat "sensibly," choose foods that provide not only fat but other essential nutrients (e.g., protein and Wber, vitamins, and minerals). Examples include nuts, seeds, avocados, whole grains, and soy.

◆ *What is trans fat?*

Trans fat is a form of dietary fat that occurs naturally in animal and dairy sources and is also man made. The leading source of trans fat comes from partially hydrogenated oils. Trans fat is found in many deep-fried foods, processed prepackaged items, pastries, cakes, cookies, chips, crackers, vegetable oils, shortenings, margarine, and reduced-fat products.

Trans fat is created during a process aimed at stabilizing polyunsaturated fats in an effort to prevent them from becoming rotten, therefore extending their shelf life. This process also helps to keep foods solid at room temperature. To do this, food manufacturers add hydrogen in a process

TABLE 4-7. Sources, Functions, and Recommended Servings of Saturated Fat★

Sources	**Animal:** Meat, poultry, dairy (milk, yogurt, and cheese), butter, and lard **Plant:** Tropical oils (palm, coconut, and cocoa butter)
Function	Stimulates the production of cholesterol by the body (total cholesterol and LDL).
Recom-mendations	Substituting unsaturated fat for saturated fat in the diet is optimal to reduce cholesterol and provide your body with the essential nutrients only dietary fat can produce, including essential fatty acids (omega 3 and 6) and the fat-soluble vitamins A, D, E, and K.

★Leading experts recommend that saturated fat comprise 8% to 10% of your total calorie intake per day.

TABLE 4-8. Sources, Functions, and Recommended Servings of Polyunsaturated Fat★

Nutrient	Omega 3 fatty acids	Omega 6 fatty acids
Sources	Soybean oil, marine fish (salmon, herring, albacore tuna, and mackerel)	Vegetable oils (corn, safflower, sunflower, soybean, cotton-seed, sesame), leafy green vegetables, nuts, seeds, and whole grains
Function	May reduce blood tri-glycerides, blood pressure, platelet aggregation, and clot formation.	May reduce total cholesterol and low-density lipoprotein (LDL) when substituted for saturated fat in the diet.

★Leading experts recommend that polyunsaturated fat comprise up to 10% of your total calorie intake per day.

TABLE 4-9. Sources, Functions and Recommended Servings of Monounsaturated Fat★

Sources	Olive, canola, and peanut oils; avocados; and most nuts (macadamia, pecans, almonds, cashews and hazelnuts).
Function	When substituted for saturated fat, monounsaturated fat has a neutral to mildly lowering effect on cholesterol.

★Research has suggested that high-density lipoprotein (HDL) levels remain unchanged and/or slightly raised with consumption of mono-unsaturated fat in place of saturated fat.

TABLE 4-10. Recommended Grams of Fat Based on Total Calorie Intake★

Total Calories per day	Total fat (grams)	Saturated fat (grams)	Unsaturated fat (grams)
1200	27–40	<13	<27
1300	29–43	<14	<29
1400	31–47	<16	<31
1500	33–50	<17	<33
1600	36–53	<18	<36
1700	38–57	<19	<38
1800	40–60	<20	<40
1900	42–63	<21	<42
2000	44–67	<22	<44
2100	47–70	<23	<47
2200	49–73	<24	<49
2300	51–77	<26	<51
2400	53–80	<27	<53
2500	56–83	<28	<56
2600	58–87	<29	<58
2700	60–90	<30	<60
2800	62–93	<31	<62
2900	64–97	<32	<64
3000	67–100	<33	<67
3100	69–103	<34	<69

★This is only a guide.

known as hydrogenation. This process chemically converts polyunsaturated fat to trans fat. If you see the word "partially hydrogenated" on the food label, it is likely that the product has trans fat in it.

Research has suggested that trans fat, which is similar to saturated fat, may increase total cholesterol and reduce high-density lipoprotein (HDL). Additionally, trans fat may increase triglycerides.

Leading experts recommend:

- Consuming fats in the whole and natural form whenever possible (especially from unsaturated sources)
- Limiting the amount of prepackaged, processed, and fast food
- Reading food labels and recognizing the source of fat

◈ *What is cholesterol?*

Cholesterol is a soft, fat-like, waxy substance present in all parts of the body. Cholesterol is available from two sources: your body (made in the liver) and your diet (found in animal foods only). Research has suggested that cholesterol in food is not the primary source of high blood cholesterol for most individuals. Rather, saturated fat tends to raise blood cholesterol to a greater degree.

Dietary cholesterol is only found in foods made of animal products. Sources of dietary cholesterol include the following:

- Meat
  3 ounces (10% fat)—75 milligrams (mg) cholesterol
- Poultry
  3 ounces white breast meat—66 mg cholesterol
  3 ounces dark meat—75 mg cholesterol
- Eggs
  1 whole egg—230 mg cholesterol
  2 egg whites—0 mg cholesterol
- Milk
  1 cup whole milk—34 mg cholesterol
  1 cup skim (non-fat) milk—4 mg cholesterol
- Yogurt
  1 cup low-fat yogurt—12 mg cholesterol
- Cheese
  1.5 ounces cheddar cheese—44 mg cholesterol
  1.5 ounces part-skim mozzarella cheese—23 mg cholesterol
- Fish
  3 ounces tuna—54 mg cholesterol
- Shellfish
  3 ounces shrimp—129 mg cholesterol
- Butter
  1 tablespoon—31 mg cholesterol

Leading experts recommend that you eat 300 milligrams or less of cholesterol per day.

Limiting Sugars

Experts recommend that less than 10% of your total calories come from refined and added sugar. Sugar may raise your blood triglyceride levels. Refined and added sugar is found in cakes, cookies, candies, sodas, table sugar, honey, etc., and is a source of empty calories. These foods provide energy for your body to function; however, they lack the essential nutrients such as vitamins, minerals, phytochemicals, and dietary fiber that your body needs to function at its best. When deciding how to best nourish yourself, remember that your body needs a variety of nutrients each day. Use the Food Guide Pyramid as a guide to shape your eating patterns.

Fat-free foods often have increased amounts of sugar and just as many calories as the original food. Unfortunately, fat free does not mean calorie free. For example, a can of soda is fat free, but it can have ten teaspoons (40 g.) of sugar. Always check food labels, since sugar may be in foods that you would not normally think of as being sweetened.

> "I have never had a problem about eating since I was a kid. I mean, I think I was conditioned for that because my mother and dad both were good cooks. I think I am conditioned to appreciate eating."
>
> *Heart attack survivor*

Limiting Salt

Salt is composed of sodium and chloride. Sodium is a nutrient that our body needs every day. It controls and maintains the volume of blood in our body and our blood pressure. However, too much sodium causes the body to hold onto more fluid, increasing the blood volume and pressure.

Sodium comes from three sources:

- 15% occurs in the foods we eat
- 35% comes from common table salt
- 50% comes from processed foods

◆ *How can I decrease the sodium in my food plan?*

- Remove the salt shaker from the table. Try a salt-free herb mixture to season your food (see Exhibits 4-11 through 4-13).
- Use "lite salt," which contains 50% sodium and 50% potassium. Lite salt in place of regular will decrease your overall salt intake.
- When cooking, decrease or eliminate the salt. Try using spices,

low-sodium broth, pepper, lemon juice, or flavored vinegar to season food.

- Remember that garlic salt, onion salt, celery salt, seasoning salt, and "lite salt" all contain salt. Lemon pepper and bouillon may also contain salt. Remember to read the labels even on spices. Use garlic powder, onion powder, celery seed, or salt-free seasonings.

EXHIBIT 4-11. Herb Blend for "Salt Shakers"

2 tsp. thyme leaves
2 tsp. ground savory
1 tsp. rubbed sage
2 tsp. basil leaves
1 Tbsp. marjoram leaves
Mix all ingredients and grind together in a blender, food processor, or mortar and pestle. Store in a tightly covered glass jar. Use in place of salt at the table, and for cooking.

Reprinted with permission from Creative Salt-free Seasonings from McCormick/Schilling.

Avoid highly processed meats and cheeses such as cured, smoked, and canned meats.

- Remember that many sauces are high in sodium (such as soy

EXHIBIT 4-12. Herb Blend for Stews, Soups, Chicken or Pot Roast

1 Tbsp. thyme leaves
1 Tbsp. marjoram leaves
1 tsp. rubbed sage
2 tsp. rosemary leaves
Mix all ingredients and grind together in blender, food processor or mortar and pestle. Store in tightly covered glass jar. Use in place of salt for cooking or sprinkle over cooked foods.

Reprinted with permission from Creative Salt-free Seasonings from McCormick/Schilling.

---

sauce, barbecue sauce, marinades, steak sauce, teriyaki sauce, and dry sauce mixtures).
- Choose fresh and frozen vegetables instead of canned vegetables.
- Limit pickled items and vegetables stored in brine, as these are very high in salt.
- Limit convenience foods such as frozen dinners, canned entrees, packaged rice and pasta mixes, and fast foods. Try making rice with fresh vegetables and herbs.

EXHIBIT 4-13. Meat and Vegetable Seasoning Blend

1 tsp. celery seed	1 Tbsp. marjoram leaves
1 tsp. thyme leaves	1 Tbsp. basil leaves
1 tsp. onion powder	

Combine ingredients and keep tightly covered in a jar. Shake well before using. Sprinkle lightly over beef or vegetables before cooking.

Reprinted with permission from Creative Salt-free Seasonings from McCormick/Schilling.

Limiting Alcoholic Beverages

While some researchers have reported benefits from drinking alcohol, increasing your alcohol consumption may also increase other risks for you. Check with your doctor before drinking alcohol. This is especially important if you are taking any type of medication.

Part 4

Nutrition and Cardiovascular Health—What Else Should I Know?

Soy, Homocysteine, and Flaxseed

◆ *What is soy?*

Soy is rich in soluble and insoluble fiber and omega 3 fatty acids, and it provides all the essential amino acids. Soy also contains some natural estrogen, which may decrease hot flashes in postmenopausal women. It is the most complete plant protein. Leading experts suggest that 25 grams of soy per day, as part of a diet low in saturated fat, may reduce the risk of coronary artery disease. Soy may benefit the heart by:

- Lowering blood cholesterol and possibly triglycerides
- Decreasing blood clotting and reducing the risk of a heart attack and stroke.
- Contributing to vascular health by promoting widening of the arteries under stress and decreasing the process of low-density lipoprotein (LDL) formation in the blood vessels.
- Decreasing intake of saturated fat and cholesterol (if used to replace some of the animal protein in the diet).

Sources of soy include miso, soybeans, soy nuts, soy flour, soy milk, tofu, tempeh, and textured soy protein. Dietary protein should come from a variety of sources, not just soy.

◆ What is homocysteine?

Homocysteine is an amino acid that is produced in the human body. Elevated levels of homocysteine in the blood may harm the lining of the arteries and contribute to blood clotting. Excessive levels are thought to result from a lack of vitamins: folic acid, B6, and B12. Good sources of folic acid include avocados, bananas, orange juice, dry fortified cereal, asparagus, fruits, green leafy vegetables, dried beans and peas, and yeast. Good sources of vitamin B6 include lean meat, fish, poultry, whole grains, dry fortified cereals, soybeans, avocados, baked potatoes with skins, watermelons, and bananas. Good sources of vitamin B12 include lean meat, dairy products (milk, yogurt and cheese), eggs, and fish. Vitamin B12 is found only in animal products. However, some manufacturers have begun to fortify dry cereal with this vitamin.

◆ What is flaxseed?

Flax is a blue, flowering plant containing seeds rich in oil. Flaxseed provides a wealth of nutrients including protein, essential fatty acids (omega 3 and 6), vitamins and minerals, and soluble and insoluble fiber. Flaxseed is naturally low in saturated fat and provides unsaturated fat, especially the essential fatty acid omega 3, to the diet. Omega 3 fatty acids may assist in modifying several risk factors associated with cardiovascular disease, including the reduction of triglycerides and the lowering of blood pressure. Omega 3 fatty acids may prevent blood platelets from clotting and sticking to artery walls.

Sources of flax include grounded flaxseed, flaxseed oil, and flaxseed flour. No current recommendation exists for the amount of flax in the diet. However, including flax in your diet not only can add enjoyable flavor, but also can help bring your diet in line with current nutritional recommendations to help reduce the risk of cardiovascular disease.

Part 5

Grocery Store Nutrition

◆ *What information do I need to know when looking at food labels?*

Since 1994, nearly all packaged foods have been required to carry an accurate food label. Nutrition information for fresh fruits, vegetables, and meats is not required by law but is often voluntarily posted in the respective areas of the store. The following tips will help you understand food labels and allow you to make more healthful food choices:

- Be aware of portion sizes. Remember that nutrient values are listed per serving. If the serving size you are going to eat is not the same as the serving size on the label, you will need to adjust the nutrient values to determine what applies to you.
- Limit your total fat grams to 3 grams of fat per 100 calories.
- Know that percentages of daily values printed on a food label are based on a 2,000- or 2,500-calorie diet and may not apply to you.
- You can calculate the percentage of calories from fat in a food by

$$\text{Percentage of calories for fat} = \frac{\text{Calories from fat}}{\text{Total calories}}$$

$$\text{Example:} \quad \frac{100}{400} = 0.25 \ (25\%)$$

dividing calories from fat by total calories.

The sample food label in Figure 4-4 will help you study the different items which can be used to determine calories of fat per portion size and other important factors for healthful eating.

◆ *Can I believe food claims such as "low fat," "light," and "cholesterol free"?*

You can believe the food claims on the labels. The descriptive terms used are regulated by the government and have standard definitions. Table 4-11 outlines a few of the more common terms used by food and beverage

FIGURE 4-4. Sample Food Label

Nutrition Facts Serving Size about 3 Tbsp Serving Per Container: about 2.5	
Amount per serving as packaged	
Calories	170
Calories from fat	100
	% Daily Value★
Total Fat 11 g	**17%**
Saturated fat 2.5 g	**12%**
Cholesterol 0 mg	**0%**
Sodium 390 mg	**16%**
Total Carbohydrate 19 g	**6%**
Dietary Fiber 4 g	**15%**
Protein 3 g	

Vitamin A 0% • Vitamin C 0% • Calcium 2% • Iron 4% • Sugar 0%

★Percent daily values are based on a 2,000-calorie diet. Your daily values may be higher or lower depending on your calorie needs:

		Calories: 2,000	2,500
Total Fat	Less than	65 g	80 g
Sat Fat	Less than	20 g	25 g
Cholesterol	Less than	300 mg	300 mg
Sodium	Less than	2,400 mg	2,400 mg
Total Carbohydrate		300 g	375 g
Dietary Fiber		25 g	30 g

Calories per gram:
Fat 9 • Carbohydrate 4 • Protein 4

companies.

◆ *Should I read the ingredient list? What should I look for?*

TABLE 4-11. Claims on Food Labels

Food Label Claim	Definition
Fat free	Less than 0.5 grams of fat per serving
Cholesterol free	Less than 2 milligrams of cholesterol and 2 grams or less of saturated fat
Low sodium	140 milligrams or less of sodium
Low calorie	40 calories or less
Reduced	25% less of the item listed than found in the regular product

You can learn about a food product by reading the ingredient list. Ingredients are listed in order of descending amounts. The main ingredient is listed first and the smallest ingredient last. If fat, sodium, or sugar is listed among the first few ingredients, you may wish to choose this food prod-

TABLE 4-12. Ingredients That Are Sources of Sodium, Fat, and Sugar

Sodium	Fat	Sugar
Any ingredient with the word "sodium"	Bacon fat	Barley malt
Baking powder	Beef fat	Brown sugar
Baking soda	Butter	Cane sugar
Bouillon	Chicken fat	Corn sweetener
Brine	Cocoa butter	Dextrose
Monosodium glutamate	Coconut oil	Fructose
Salt (sodium chloride)	Cream sauce	Glucose
Sea kelp	Hydrogenated vegetable oil	Grape sugar
Sea salt	Lard	Honey
Sodium nitrate	Meat fat	Maltose
Sodium saccharin	Palm	Manitol
Soy sauce	Palm kernel oil	Molasses
	Pork fat	Sorbitol
	Shortening	Sucrose
	Sour cream	
	Whole milk solids	

uct less often. Table 4-12 will assist you in being aware of names for sodium, fat, and sugar sources.

◆ What foods do I need to buy?

The first step in deciding what foods to buy is to remember that there are no "good" or "bad" foods. All foods can fit into a sensible and balanced eating plan. You will want to keep in mind the guidelines discussed in Part 1 when eating out, preparing food, and shopping. The first several grocery lists and shopping trips you plan will take some time, but before you know it you will be an expert at making nutritious choices. The following lists will assist you with making your choices.

Meat, poultry, fish, and protein foods
- Extra lean and lean meat with less than 10% fat
- Lean meat such as "round" or "loin."—examples include top round, top loin, round tip, eye of round, sirloin, tenderloin
- Canadian bacon instead of bacon
- Skinless, boneless chicken or turkey breast
- Ground turkey or chicken breast (without skin)
- Fresh fish fillets such as salmon, cod, halibut, flounder, orange roughy, and red snapper
- Fresh or frozen shrimp, crab, or lobster
- Canned, water-packed albacore tuna, salmon, or sardines
- Dried beans, peas, and lentils (kidney beans, lima beans, pinto beans, black-eyed beans, chick-peas)
- Tofu (soybean curd)
- Nuts, seeds, and natural peanut butter

Milk and dairy products
- 1% or skim (non-fat) milk (or soy milk for a non-dairy choice)
- Non-fat, dry, or evaporated skim milk
- Low-fat yogurt
- Cheeses labeled low fat, part-skim, or made with skim milk

Breads, cereals, and grain products
- Whole-grain breads such as whole wheat, oat rye, and pumpernickel
- Whole-grain bagels, English muffins, and pita bread
- Corn or flour tortillas (made with vegetable oil)
- Whole-grain crackers, breadsticks, Melba toast, and crisp breads
- Whole grains such as bulgur, couscous, kasha, millet, and quinoa
- Pasta, brown rice, and basmati rice

- Hot cereals (i.e., oats, cream of wheat, cream of rice, grits, etc.)
- Dry cereals made from whole grains, such as shredded wheat, oat squares, and bran flakes

Vegetables and fruits
- Fresh and frozen vegetables and fruits. If selecting canned vegetables, look for "no salt added"
- Canned fruits packed in their own juices
- 100% fruit juices
- Dried fruits (apples, raisins, cranberries, apricots, berries, mango, etc.)

Snack items and beverages
- Air-popped popcorn
- Baked chips with humus or bean dip
- Graham crackers, whole grain snack mixes or whole grain crackers with low-fat cheese or natural peanut butter
- Part-skim mozzarella sticks or low-fat yogurts
- Fresh fruits and vegetables or trail mixes (dried fruit and nuts)
- Beverages: caffeine-free coffee, seltzers, caffeine-free herbal teas, and club soda

Condiments and oils
- Flavored vinegar (such as balsamic), fresh herbs and spices, lemon juice, jelly, mustard, salsa, bean dip, low-sodium bouillon, and oil-based salad dressing
- Canola, olive, safflower, cottonseed, corn, and vegetable oils
- Non-stick cooking sprays
- Soft tub or squeeze margarine (look for items without trans fat)

Making changes in stages will be easier than trying to change everything at once. You might want to start with a different group each week to give yourself time to get used to your new eating habits. You might want to plan your menus for the week and make your shopping list based on your goals. Shopping with a prepared list may help you avoid buying things on impulse. A helpful tip is to not go grocery shopping when you are hungry. This will help you to avoid selecting choices that are not on your list.

Part 6

Recipe Modification

◈ *Do I need to throw away all of my recipes?*

TABLE 4-13. Suggested Substitutions in Recipes

Instead of	Use
Whole milk	Skim, non-fat, or 1% milk or low-fat buttermilk
Heavy cream	Evaporated skim milk, or fat-free half-and-half
Cream/non-dairy	Non-fat powdered milk
Canned cream soups	Homemade cream soup recipe: In a saucepan, use a whisk to stir together 1 cup of evaporated skim milk, 1 tsp. cornstarch and 1tsp. instant low-sodium bouillon. Cook and stir until thickened and bubbly.
Sour cream	Light or non-fat sour cream or low-fat plain yogurt. If yogurt is to be heated, add 1 Tbsp. cornstarch to 1 cup yogurt to prevent separation. Or take 1 cup low-fat cottage cheese and mix it in a blender.
Whipped cream	Chilled evaporated skim milk: whip milk and stir in 1 tsp. lemon juice. Or try low fat whipped cream.
Whole eggs	Two egg whites or ¼ cup egg substitute in place of each whole egg.
High-fat cheese	Low-fat, skim milk cheese, or cheese with less than 5 grams of fat per ounce. Tips for using reduced or fat-free cheese in cooking: • Shred the cheese finely • When making sauces and soups, toss the cheese with a small amount of flour, cornstarch, or arrowroot.
Mayonnaise	Use light or fat-free mayonnaise or mix equal parts of non-fat plain yogurt with mayonnaise to make creamy lower-fat dressing for tuna or chicken salad.
Butter or shortening for greasing pans	Non-stick vegetable spray.
High-fat meats	Ground turkey or chicken breast in dishes that call for ground meat. Try lean cuts of meat, such as sirloin. Remove the skin from chicken and turkey.

TABLE 4-13. Suggested Substitutions in Recipes (continued)

Instead of	Use
Butter, shortening, or lard	Margarine (tub style) or vegetable oil: When replacing solid fat with liquid oil, ¾ cup of liquid can be used in place of 1 cup of solid. When baking, you can often replace fat with fruit such as applesauce or puréed prunes or pears. For example, if a recipe calls for ½ cup oil, use ½ cup applesauce instead. Puréed prunes are great in chocolate baked goods.
Sugar	In recipes for baked products, the sugar can be reduced by ¼ or ⅓ without changing the final product. Using cinnamon or vanilla will help add sweetness.
Unsweetened baking	For each ounce of unsweetened chocolate needed, use 3 Tbsp. unsweetened cocoa powder plus 1 Tbsp. oil.
Salt	No salt (eliminate it from the recipe) unless it is used as a leavening agent. (A leavening agent is something that helps a baked product rise evenly.)

You do not need to throw out all of your favorite recipes. You can significantly decrease calories, cholesterol, sodium, and fat by modifying your recipes with available healthful products. Table 4-13 will give you great tips and recommendations.

◈ Are there any cookbooks with healthful foods that also have great-tasting recipes?

Many cookbooks have healthful recipes. The following list offers some excellent titles, but there are many others available.

- *American Heart Association Low-Fat, Low Cholesterol Cookbook: Heart Healthy, Easy-to-Make Recipes That Taste Great* (American Heart Association)
- *Around the World Cookbook: Healthy Recipes with International Flavor* (American Heart Association)
- *The Art of Cooking for the Diabetic,* 3rd Edition (Mary Abbott Hess)
- *Betty Crocker's Low-Fat Low-Cholesterol Cookbook* (Betty Crocker Home Library)

- *The Complete Soy Cookbook* (Paulette Mitchell)
- *Healthy Cooking for Two* (Brenda Shiver and Angela Shiver)
- *In the Kitchen with Rosie* (Rosie Daley, Oprah Winfrey)
- *1001 Low-Fat Recipes,* 2nd Edition (Sue Spitler and Linda R. Yoakam)
- *Magic Menus* (American Diabetes Association)
- *Moosewood Restaurant Low-Fat Recipes* (Moosewood Collective)
- *Quick and Easy Cookbook* (American Heart Association)
- *Quick and Healthy Low-Fat Cooking, Featuring All-American Food* (Jean Rogers, *Prevention Magazine*)

Part 7

Creating a Plan for Dining Out

> "I never have cared that much for cooking, but I love to eat."
>
> *Heart attack survivor*

◆ *If I am eating a healthful diet, can I still eat out?*

When eating out at your favorite restaurant, consider your food choices and portion sizes. Also, you may want to discuss how certain foods are prepared and what ingredients are used in your selections. If you eat out frequently, you need to be familiar with the information provided in this chapter. Occasional splurges of high-fat or high-calorie foods will not wreck your entire healthful eating plan. The key to an overall healthful food plan is to make balanced choices and to use moderation.

◆ *Are there any tips for me to remember when ordering from a menu?*

Key phrases can help identify healthful selections from restaurant menus. For example:
- Low-fat menu items are usually described as steamed, in its own juices (au jus), garden fresh, broiled, roasted, or poached.
- High-fat menu items may be described as buttered, in butter sauce, sautéed, fried, crispy, braised, creamed, in its own gravy (au jus), hollandaise, au gratin, parmesan, scalloped, casserole, prime, hash, pot pie, marinated (in oil), stewed, or basted (in oil).
- Menu items high in sodium may be described as pickled, pickled in cocktail sauce, smoked, in broth, or in a tomato base.

You may want to ask the restaurant staff or servers the following questions about menu items:

- Can you use skim or low-fat milk in that sauce?
- What is the portion size of the meat, fish, or poultry?
- Will you serve the butter, dressing, gravy, or sauces in a side dish?
- Do you prepare the dish without added salt or monosodium glutamate (MSG)?
- Can you prepare special requests if I call in advance (for example, when flying)?

TABLE 4-14. Recommendations When Dining Out.

Salad Bar	• Choose plain fruits and vegetables. • Use only a small amount of dressing on salads. Try dipping your fork in the dressing and then take a bite of salad instead of pouring the dressing all over the salad. • Try using raisins instead of bacon bits; avocados, nuts, seeds or chow-mein noodles.
Buffet/Cafeteria	• Watch out for "all you can eat." • Plan your meal before going down the line. • Reduce the amount of added sauces, gravy, etc.
Italian	• Choose pasta with marinara or marsala sauce. • Limit breaded and sautéed items and cream sauce.
Mexican	• Choose salsa and pica-de-gallo. • Choose corn tortillas instead of chips. • Try fajitas and plain beans. • Reduce the amount of dips, guacamole, sour cream, and queso.
Oriental	• Eat steamed rice. • Try foods that are boiled, steamed, or stir-fried.
Steak/Seafood	• Reduce the portion size of steak or seafood to 3–4 ounces per serving. • Try a baked potato instead of steak fries. Watch the amount of butter and sour cream.
Pizza	• Try vegetable toppings. • Try thin crust with reduced cheese.
Airplane menus	• Request a low-fat or vegetarian meal when you make your reservation. • Drink a glass of water for every hour in the flight to help minimize jet lag.

◆ *What are some healthful dining out possibilities at different types of restaurants?*

You do not have to avoid a particular restaurant because you think it offers only high-fat choices. Instead, choose the lower sodium, calorie, and fat items provided at many restaurants. Table 4-14 provides suggestions and recommendations that will help you make good decisions when dining out.

After carefully reading through the information and recommendations in this nutrition chapter, you are prepared to take the next steps in your plan. It is recommended that you refer to specific questions or suggestions made in this chapter as you create your first few shopping lists or plan your selection at a favorite restaurant. It is a good idea to discuss your nutrition choices with your doctor and a registered dietitian.

5

Balancing Your Life

Part I

Perspective

You have just had a major physical setback. Do you view this as an opportunity or a roadblock, a fresh start or a bad change, a beginning or an end, an open door or a closed one? Most of us have heard the question "Is your glass half empty or half full?" but have you associated this question with your diagnosis of cardiovascular disease? You may be trying to adjust to a more healthful lifestyle and also feel saddened by the fact that you need to change some things. If you have been diagnosed with cardiovascular disease, this chapter is meant not to minimize your health problems, but to discuss some of the reactions you may experience in order to help you readjust your lifestyle in a positive fashion.

> **"Change is like a supersonic train and you have three choices. You can step in front of it and refuse to move and let it run you over. You can step back and watch it pass you by. Or you can get on board and ride it, then eventually move to the front and drive it."**
>
> *Willie Jolley, author of* A Setback Is a Setup for a Comeback

Many of you may be unhappy about your health. Others of you who recently survived a major health event may be joyful for a second chance at life. Many feelings are associated with cardiovascular disease. Look at Table 5-1 and see if you have had any of the feelings listed. Have you had other feelings that are not listed?

> **"I think once you have had a heart attack it takes you a while to keep from being scared."**
>
> *Heart attack survivor*

Although these feelings are common for you and your family members after a heart event, the negative feelings should decrease with time. If problems with negative feelings continue over a long period of time, you should talk to your doctor.

TABLE 5-1. Normal Feelings Associated with Cardiovascular Disease

Feeling	Description
Fear	You may be afraid that the event may happen again.
Depression	You may feel "blue" and not care about things that you usually care about, or experiennce feelings of hopelessness.
Frustration	You may wonder: *Why can't they tell me exactly why this happened?*
Denial	You may think: *Nothing is wrong; they fixed me.*
Anger	You may feel that your situation is not fair.
Guilt	You may wonder if you did something to cause yourself to have cardiovascular disease.
Grief	You may be sad about some of the changes you are being asked to make now that you have cardiovascular disease.
Confusion	You may think: *What does all this mean and to whom should I listen?*
Joy	You may feel happy and think: *I survived!*
Thankfulness	You may be thankful for life and feel as if you have been given a second chance.
Increased motivation	You may be motivated to make necessary changes you have been putting off.

Part 2

Stress vs. Stress Management

When placed in a stressful situation, some people respond in a positive way while others simply react to the situation at hand. How do you respond? Does it depend on the situation? Would you respond differently to being late to meet a friend for dinner than if you were in an automobile accident and broke your arm? The answer is likely to be yes. Furthermore, if you had a cast on your writing hand, you would probably figure out a way to adjust so that you would not have to rely solely on oral communication for six weeks.

Many adjustments must be made when a person is diagnosed with cardiovascular disease. What did you do

> **"I might be down for a moment, but I am not out! I want to let the world know; I shall bounce back and I am coming back!"**
>
> *Willie Jolley, Author of* A Setback is a Setup for a Comeback

when you were first diagnosed with cardiovascular disease? Did you gather all the information you could find to learn how to live a more healthful life and take action, or did you decide that there was nothing you could do about it, so why bother? When there is a stressful situation before you, you might not be able to control the situation, but you can certainly control your reaction.

TABLE 5-2. Examples of Positive and Negative Stressors

Positive stressors	Negative stressors
Birth of a baby/grandbaby Holidays Promotion at work or new job Retirement Vacations Weddings	Death of a friend or family member Divorce Financial problems Injury to yourself, a friend, or family member Loss of health Loss of job

◆ *What is a stressful situation?*

Stress is defined differently depending on what dictionary you are reading. Some dictionaries define stress as either positive or negative. For the purpose of this book, the definition used in *Mosby's Medical Dictionary* (3rd Edition, 1990) will serve as the definition of stress, which is "any change that results in an adjustment." Stress, therefore, is not always negative, as many people believe it to be. It is a constant series of reactions to the changes in our world and, more personally, in our life. *Eustress* is the technical name for positive stress and *distress* is used to describe negative stress. For the remainder of this chapter, however, the generic term "stress" will be used, since the reaction to stress is what we will focus on. Just keep in mind that stress can be either positive or negative (Table 5-2). For example, some people may react poorly to what is normally considered a positive change, such as a baby or grandbaby being born. The fact that this is generally considered a happy event does not mean that it comes without adjustments. However, research shows that people are better able to handle changes that they have chosen.

◆ Do stressful situations affect me physically?

A stressor is defined in *Mosby's Medical Dictionary* (3rd Edition, 1990) as "anything that causes wear and tear on the body's physical or mental resources." When looking at the amount of stress you have had in your life, it is important to combine both positive and negative stressors to determine the total amount of stress you have had. It is also important to remember that stress is cumulative—in other words, you need to look at the amount of stress you have experienced over the period of the last year.

Long-term stress and illness are related (Table 5-3). The physical long-term stress response affects your immune system and leaves you less able to fight disease. For example, have you ever acquired a cold or sore throat when you were under a deadline at work or up many nights in a row caring for a sick relative? These ailments might have been your body's reaction to the stress. If you can train yourself to be flexible when it comes to life changes, you might be able to reduce your chance of illness.

Your body prepares itself for battle when placed in a stressful situation. It decides whether to run from the "enemy" or to fight it. This is called the fight or flight response. Your body responds to emotional stress the same way it does to a physical crisis. Therefore, a dog chasing you, a driver cutting you off in traffic, or the long line in the grocery store might all activate your fight or flight response. An average person may have this response anywhere from 30 to 50 times a day.

◆ What is the difference between short-term and long-term stress?

Look at the diagram of the human body that shows some physical re-

FIGURE 5-1. Stress Responses

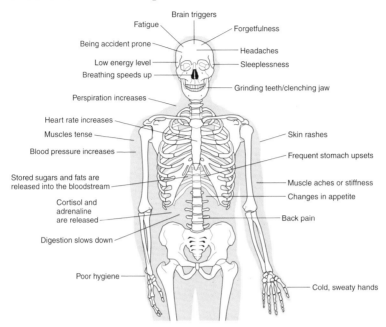

sponses to stress (Figure 5-1). Can you imagine that frequent repetitions of these responses would be harmful to your body?

Short-Term Stress: The Healthful Kind

In the short-term stress graph, the "uh-oh" is the stressor and the "whew" is what you do to soothe or reduce it, depending on what the stressor is. The "uh-oh" may be a red traffic light when you are in a hurry, and the "whew" the fact that you were able to turn right on red and take a different route. It is important to note that what is effective for reducing one person's stress may not work for someone else. Let's examine the traffic light scenario: Susie chooses to drive out of her way to avoid it, Bob yells at it, Stephen decides not to be bothered by it, Jo Anne turns right on red, Phyllis shakes a fist at the world, and Judy drives straight through it. Whatever your individual reaction is, ideally it should safely return you to your baseline stress level.

Short-term stress may result in the following physical and emotional responses:

- Increased heart rate
- Increased blood pressure
- Faster breathing
- Increased perspiration
- Increased muscle tension
- Slowed digestion
- Release of cortisol and adrenaline
- Release of stored sugars and fats into the bloodstream

Table 5-3 lists additional side effects of stress.

TABLE 5-3. Side Effects of Stress

Physical side effects	Your mood can be affected with	Your behavior can be altered with
Back pain	Anxiety	Being accident prone
Changes in appetite	Frustration	Clinching jaw
Cold, sweaty hands	Increased anger	Emotional outbursts
Fatigue	Increased hostility	Forgetfulness
Frequent stomach	Irritability	Grinding teeth
upsets	Lack of interest in	Inability to
Headaches	your normal activities	concentrate
Low energy level	Restlessness	Poor hygiene
Muscle aches or		Sleeplessness
stiffness		
Skin rashes		

Source:1996 Hospital Educators Resource Catalogue, Inc.

Long-Term Stress: The Hazardous Kind

Long-term stress usually involves one "uh-oh" after another without a stress reliever or "whew" (Figure 5-2). In this situation, since the stress level has not been reduced, it can become dangerously high. Without the "whew," the short-term stress response stays activated and the stress chemicals continue to be dumped into the bloodstream. The short-term physical responses are prolonged and the long-term responses are added. This long-term stress may put our bodies into a "crisis mode," making us at risk for illness. For example, picture a wife and her 30-year-old daughter taking care of their severely ill husband/father who has been in the hospital for a month. The wife and daughter trade off sleeping at the hospital every night and are there all day with him. When other family members offer to help, they refuse stating they are "doing fine." When their loved

FIGURE 5-2. Long-Term Stress—Unhealthful

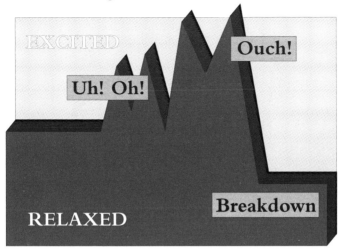

one passes on, both the wife and daughter become sick themselves. As time passes, they both acknowledge that they should have allowed family and friends to help them during his extended illness, but they did not. They also feel strongly that the long-term stress they had been under had contributed to their illnesses.

The following physical and emotional responses can occur when experiencing long-term stress that has led to a crisis mode:

- Depressed immune system
- Increased gastric acid
- Possible increased cholesterol and triglycerides

The Even Keel

The "even keel" is the goal in reducing stress. When looking at Figure 5-3, The Even Keel, notice that for every "uh-oh" there is a "whew" to help you relieve the stress and relax. When you wake up in the mornings, you are at your baseline stress level for that particular day. Ideally, your stress level should be no higher when you go to bed than it was when you woke up. However, as many of us experience stressors, we do not create a "whew" to bring us back to our baseline stress level. This results in a build up of stress throughout the day, which ends up in a higher stress level when we go to bed, and results in a higher baseline stress level the next day. The key is to stop the stress cycle so that there is a "whew" for most, if not all, stressors.

FIGURE 5-3. Healthful Stress—Even Keel

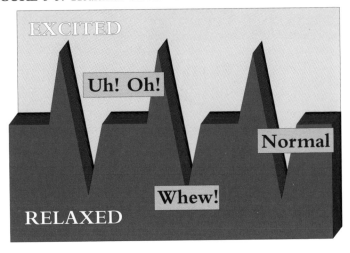

If you think it is impossible to create a "whew" for every stressor that you face in a day, you'll be surprised to learn that a "whew" might be as small as taking a deep breath and closing your eyes for a moment. If this technique works for you, it might be enough to bring your stress level down and get you closer to the even keel.

Take a minute to fill out the questionnaire in Table 5-4. It will help you analyze your stressors over the past year.

◆ What does my score on the Recent Life Changes Questionnaire mean?

The Recent Life Changes Questionnaire lists 74 life change events that potentially could occur in your life. According to the authors, if you filled out the questionnaire based on the past six months, a score of 300 or more indicates a high level of recent life stress. If you filled out the questionnaire based on the past year, a score of 500 or more indicates high stress (Miller, 1997).

There is a relationship between long-term stress and illness. The higher your score on the questionnaire, the more potential you have to become ill. The long-term stress response affects the immune system and leaves you less able to fight disease. However, it is important to know that the questionnaire in Table 5-4 measures only the changes in our lives, not the adjustments we make to those changes. In other words, if we can learn to adjust more positively to stressors and changes as they happen, we may reduce the likelihood of illness.

TABLE 5-4. Recent Life Changes Questionnaire

INSTRUCTIONS: Determine which of the following life events have happened to you in the past year. Indicate all changes, regardless of whether you view them as positive or negative. Circle the score next to the categories that apply to you. Add up the point values of those events to achieve your overall score.

Score	Category
	HEALTH
	An injury or illness which:
74	• Kept you in bed a week or more, or in the hospital
44	• Was less serious than described above
26	Major dental work
27	Major change in eating habits
26	Major change in sleeping habits
28	Major change in usual type and/or amount of recreation
	WORK
51	Change to new type of work
35	Change in work hours and conditions
	Change in responsibilities at work:
29	• More responsibilities
21	• Fewer responsibilities
31	• Promotion
42	• Demotion
32	• Transfer
	Troubles at work:
29	• With your boss

TABLE 5-4. Recent Life Changes Questionnaire (continued)

	WORK (continued)
35	• With co-workers
35	• With persons under your supervision
28	• Other work troubles
60	Major business adjustment
52	Retirement
	Loss of job:
68	• Laid off from work
79	• Fired from work
18	Correspondence course to help you in your work
	HOME AND FAMILY
42	Major change in living conditions
	Change in residence:
25	• Move within the same town or city
47	• Move to a diVerent town, city, or state
25	Change in family get-togethers
55	Major change in health or behavior of family member
50	Marriage
67	Pregnancy
65	Miscarriage or abortion
	Gain of a new family member:
66	• Birth of a child
65	• Adoption of a child
59	• A relative moving in with you
46	Spouse beginning or ending work

TABLE 5-4. Recent Life Changes Questionnaire (continued)

	HOME AND FAMILY (continued)
	Child leaving home:
41	• To attend college
41	• Due to marriage
45	• For other reasons
50	Change in arguments with spouse
38	In-law problems
	Change in the marital status of your parents:
59	• Divorce
50	• Remarriage
	Separation from spouse:
53	• Due to work
76	• Due to marital problems
96	Divorce
43	Birth of grandchild
119	Death of spouse
	Death of other family member:
123	• Child
102	• Brother or sister
100	• Parent
	PERSONAL AND SOCIAL
26	Change in personal habits
38	Beginning or ending school or college
35	Change of school or college
24	Change in political beliefs

TABLE 5-4. Recent Life Changes Questionnaire (continued)

	PERSONAL AND SOCIAL (continued)
29	*Change in religious beliefs*
27	*Change in social activities*
24	*Vacation*
37	*New, close, personal relationship*
45	*Engegement to marry*
39	*Girlfriend or boyfriend problems*
44	*Sexual difficulties*
47	*Falling-out of a close, personal relationship*
48	*An accident*
20	*Minor violation of the law*
75	*Being held in jail*
70	*Death of a close friend*
51	*Major decision regarding your immediate future*
36	*Major personal achievement*
	FINANCIAL
	Major change in finances:
38	*• Increased income*
60	*• Decreased income*
56	*• Investment and/or credit difficulties*
43	*Loss or damage of personal property*
20	*Moderate purchase*
37	*Major purchase*
58	*Foreclosure on a mortgage or loan*
	TOTAL SCORE

Part 3

Learning to Cope

◆ *What is coping?*

Coping is defined as "a process by which a person deals with stress, solves problems, and makes decisions" (Glanze, 1990). There are two parts to coping: the thought process that allows you to identify the stressor and the automatic reactions that focus on relieving the discomfort associated with the stressor. An automatic reaction might be a tool that you use to survive the stressful situation (sometimes called a defense mechanism) which does not actually relieve the stressor. An example of a defense mechanism is blaming something on someone else instead of being accountable for your own actions.

In order to cope and be able to let go of stress, it is important to determine the cause of the stressor so you can learn how to react to it. For example, Teresa was diagnosed with diabetes 35 years ago. When she was diagnosed, she already knew that diabetes could be dangerous if not controlled and, therefore, was determined to learn all that she could in order to live with the disease. Because of her willingness to gather information and take care of herself, she has been able to lead an active life and states that she has learned to live with the disease instead of for it.

Coping with your stressors can mean doing a "self-discovery" about the event that happened by trying to find out why it occurred, how you could have prevented it (if at all), and how you are going to deal with it. In contrast, coping can be simply deciding that whatever happened is not important, and you will not dwell on it. In other words, try to begin to let go of the things that you cannot control. You may also decide to let go of the stress for the moment and come back to it when you are better able to deal with the problem. Table 5-5 describes some common coping techniques. Do you recognize any techniques that you have used in the past? As you read over the table, keep in mind that the coping technique that you choose will probably depend on the severity of the stressor.

TABLE 5-5. Common Coping Strategies

Coping strategy	Benefit
Using humor	Studies show that humor reduces pain and increases productivity.
Exercising	Relieves muscle tension and releases beta-endorphins that boost the immune system; also decreases depression and anxiety.
Changing self-talk	Allows you to recognize your negative inner critic, turn off repetitive negative messages, and replace them with neutral or positive messages.
Controlling of anger	Research shows that an individual with chronic hostility may develop a stress habit that can damage the heart (Williams, 1993; Everson, 1997).
Treating depression	A period of mild depression is normal in the weeks following a cardiac event, but research shows that depression that goes untreated may have a negative effect on the recovery process (Frasure-Smith, 1993; Blumenthal, 1997).

TABLE 5-5. Common Coping Strategies (continued)

Coping strategy	Benefit
Using relaxation techniques	Mental relaxation follows physical relaxation (and vice versa) and relieves tension. Try progressive muscle relaxation, visualization, meditation, or deep breathing. (These techniques are explained later in this chapter.)
Changing stressful beliefs	Enables you to challenge beliefs that allow repetitive stressors to get to you.
Clarifying values	Allows you to prioritize and let go of less important stressors.
Balancing your eating plan	Provides the stamina and good health to cope with stress.
Seeking and utilizing support	Avoiding social isolation can improve your physical outcome after a heart event (Berkman, 1992; King, 1997).
Making and taking leisure time	Allows you to recharge.
Letting go of perfectionism	Allows you to set more realistic expectations of yourself.
Managing your time	A planned approach to juggling the demands of work, family and life will be less stressful for you.
Being mindful	Living within the present moment without worries of yesterday or concerns for tomorrow allows you to be less stressed.

How do you respond to stress?

On a short-term basis and with a healthful response from you, stress can be good and can motivate you to do your best and handle crises. The key, however, is learning to adjust to any given stressor. It is when the stress response happens over a long period of time that it becomes bad for our health.

The term *rational emotive therapy* was created by Dr. Albert Ellis and has been described in several books including *Is It Worth Dying For* by Dr.

Robert S. Eliot and Dennis L. Breo (1989). The underlying theme of rational emotive therapy is that a person's emotions are largely determined by his or her own thought patterns and self-talk. In this theory, thinking has an influence over feeling and is described in A-B-C style.

An *activating event* (the "A" in the A-B-Cs) and a stressor are similar terms and refer to an event that gets our attention. Again, this event can be positive or negative, and in their book *Is It Worth Dying For,* Dr. Eliot and Mr. Breo describe the activating event as either internal (for example, realizing you forgot a family member's birthday) or external (for example, seeing an accident).

The "B" in the A-B-Cs stands for *belief*: What belief or interpretation do you have about the event (Exhibit 5-1)? The authors describe self-talk as having a lot to do with your beliefs, because you can have neutral, positive, or negative self-talk. For example, if you usually make your bed but on Tuesday you are running late for an appointment, your self-talk might include:

1. Oh well, I just do not have time to make the bed today (neutral).
2. It is okay if I do not make the bed. And besides, if I skip it, I will have five extra minutes to grab breakfast (positive).
3. I just do not have time to make the bed and it frustrates me, but it is my fault for not waking up on time (appropriately negative).
4. Even though no one is coming over today, not making the bed shows

---

Exhibit 5-1. An Example of Changing Your Beliefs.

Robin lives alone and has had trouble sleeping because her usually quiet, eighty-pound Labrador Retriever has been barking in the middle of the night. Robin is becoming exhausted after two nights of this and is angry at her dog since he keeps waking her up. When discussing the issue with a friend, Sam pointed out that the dog may have sensed a person outside the window and had effectively scared the person away. Since Robin had not thought of her dog's barking in this way, it helped her to realize that the barking may in fact be helpful. The next time her dog barked in the middle of the night, Robin began to change her self-talk remembering that the dog was protecting her. This allowed her to relax somewhat and not get as angry, therefore she was able to get back to sleep faster. *Although this is a simplistic example, it is meant to demonstrate that changing your beliefs may be difficult, but may also be powerful when it comes to how you react to stressors.*

---

that I do not care about how my house looks. I have to make it no matter how late it makes me (inappropriately negative).

The "C" according to Dr. Eliot and Mr. Breo is for the *consequence* of "A" and "B." The consequence is the response to your thoughts and can include feelings, physical reactions, behaviors, or a combination of the three.

Responding to a situation with inappropriate negative self-talk usually results in a high level of stress. For example, your response to not making your bed might be stress-free because of neutral or positive self-talk (you let yourself off the hook for not making the bed or you have a positive reaction be-

> **"Negative self-talks are hazardous to your health. Positive self-talks are extremely powerful and can act as prescriptions for healthy change."**
> *Dr. Robert S. Eliot, author of* **From Stress to Strength**

cause you have time to eat breakfast). On the other hand, your reaction can be stressful if your self-talk is negative: you tell yourself that you are a bad person because you do not care how your house looks; you force yourself to make the bed and you leave the house late. In this case, as you are rushing to your appointment your blood pressure and heart rate rise with each extra minute that goes by.

The important message of the A-B-Cs is that although you cannot control the events that happen in your life, you can control your beliefs, which will then control the consequences. The consequence can be stress-free, neutral, or stressful.*

◆ How do I condition myself to have a healthful response to stressors?

> **"Step back, take a deep breath, cry if necessary . . . but then get back up and get back at it."**
> *Willie Jolley, author of* **A Setback is a Setup for a Comeback**

It takes approximately 30 days to establish a new physical or emotional habit (Wetmore, 2000). You can condition yourself to have a healthful response to emotional obstacles. We may feel as if we have no control over the changes in our lives, but we do have control of how we adjust to those changes. You can

---

*This is just one example of the A-B-Cs of emotional habits. For more information, try reading *How to Keep People from Pushing Your Buttons* by A. Ellis and A. Lange (1994) or *Is It Worth Dying For* by R. S. Eliot and D. L. Breo (1989).

make conscious decisions to have a positive outlook regarding your cardiovascular disease. For example, you can get educated about it, decide on a plan of action, set goals, live life to the fullest, and get started on the road to good health—but this will take a concerted effort on your part.

◆ *What are some suggestions to follow when coping with stress?*

What works for one person may not work for another. The following survival tips may be useful when implementing your coping strategies. Can you think of instances when you might use these tips in your own life?

- Laugh
- Rest
- Diversify your interests
- Be assertive
- Clarify expectations
- Use the three Fs (friends, family, fun)
- Communicate your needs
- Seek and explore spirituality
- Share with others
- Just say no
- Set limits and tell people what they are
- Change your routine
- Say "thank you" and "maybe I'm wrong"
- Be aware of negative thoughts and try to change them

◆ *Is coping with heart disease different than coping with other kinds of stress?*

Stress comes in many forms—from a small obstacle in your day (such as a red traffic light) to a serious health problem. Obviously, your reaction to a serious health problem for you or a family member is not the same as being stuck at a red light when you are in a hurry. Also remember that each of us responds differently to various forms of stress. People coping with cardiovascular disease may experience a specific pattern of feelings. These feelings apply to patients, family members, and significant others because

> **"I wanted to come home [from the hospital]. It was in March. My family was coming in for the weekend and we had a lot of plans. There couldn't be a heart problem."**
>
> *Mary Ann McMullan, heart patient*

everyone is coping with the cardiovascular disease. See if you recognize any of the following experiences:

Loss of Control

This loss is described as feeling like things are beyond your control. This may have happened when you found out you had to be admitted to the hospital after having your stress test, when you were told you would need an angioplasty, or when you put on your hospital gown and became a patient.

Reason

It is normal to search for a reason why the disease has affected you and your family. "Why me? Why us? Why now?" These are all questions that you may have asked. It is human nature to find out why bad things happen to us so that we can avoid going through them again. The search for reasons often comes with guilt, such as *I should have made her quit smoking,*

I should have eaten better, or *I should have tried that exercise program last year.* Although it may be difficult, try to spend as little time as possible feeling guilty and redirect your energy towards making new lifestyle changes.

Immortality

Omnipotence is described as "a feeling of all-powerfulness" or feeling as if you are indestructible (Glanze, 1990). When you were a teenager, did you feel that nothing bad could ever happen to you? Many of us have a strong feeling of omnipotence as young people, and as we grow older the feeling diminishes but does not disappear altogether. For example, without a healthy dose of omnipotence, none of us would ever fly in an airplane or drive on a busy highway. After a heart experience, however, we tend to lose some of the feeling of omnipotence, and that can make us fearful and vulnerable. We may wrestle with the issue of our own death or the idea that someday we may not be as active as we would like.

Connections

After a heart event, our connections with family and friends change. Have you experienced a role reversal or role change in your family since your heart event? There may be changes in the social, work, or church organizations you belong to as you try to begin regular activities again. Advice may be offered to try to make sure that you follow new rules so that you do not have another heart event. Family and friends may try to take control just at a time when you are struggling to regain your own control. Fear of losing you may cause these changes among your loved ones.

A way to ease this time of changing connections is to be honest with your loved ones. Let them know how you are feeling from an emotional perspective, not just a physical one. For example, Ed was upset when his sons would not let him mow the grass several months after his heart attack. Even though the boys knew that the doctor had allowed Ed to mow sections at a time over a few weeks until he felt well enough to mow the entire yard, each weekend the boys would not let Ed mow at all. Ed was getting very angry with his sons because he felt that he should not have to ask their permission to mow his own grass. After all, his doctor had told him to go ahead and try it.

Ed's sons, on the other hand, thought they were doing what was best by taking on extra responsibility to allow their dad to rest. After several weeks of this, Ed finally told his sons that by mowing he felt he could begin to bring his life back to normal again and get back some of the control he had lost when he had the heart attack. Mowing was always Ed's job and, until the heart attack, Ed's sons did not want to mow the yard unless their allowance was raised to pay for what they called the "extra effort." When Ed's sons heard how he felt, they began to let him mow sections at a time like the doctor had suggested and kept a close eye on him. In the end, Ed was able to regain some sense of control and get back into the mowing habits that he enjoyed.

Part 4

Time Management—The Daily Balance

Let's analyze a typical day for a working person: at 5:30 A.M. the alarm goes off and you begin to get ready for work. You shower, blow-dry your hair, put on your makeup/shave, make the bed, iron your clothes, make breakfast for you and/or your family, feed the dog, pack a lunch, and head out the door to work. You have just experienced the first two hours of your day before you even hit rush-hour traffic. Even if you are retired you probably have a similar morning plan, except instead of heading to work you are heading elsewhere. Life is a balancing act, and the daily responsibilities that start the moment you get out of bed can all be stressors.

One of the most common problems that busy people face is managing their responsibilities in what seems like a time squeeze—there's never enough of it. Phrases like "there are not enough hours in the day" or "I just can't get everything done" are common in today's fast-paced environment. Feeling constantly under demand can contribute to both short- and long-term stress. Since we cannot add more hours to the day, how can we balance the daily demands of life with the necessity of rest and relaxation? Techniques of time management can get you started in the right direction. Time management is a set of related common-sense skills that help you use your time in the most effective and productive way possible (Mindtools, 1999).

Time management skills can help you:

- Prioritize your "to do" list
- Give you more time for relaxation and recreation
- Control distractions that waste time
- Reduce stress

◆ *How do you spend your time now?*

It can be difficult to reflect on how you spend your day and get an accurate picture. Many of us do things automatically and spend more time talking with friends or eating lunch than we can accurately recall. Keeping a log of your daily activities will allow you to find out exactly how you are spending your time. Write down every time you change activities while at home or work. Record everything from reading e-mail, attending a meeting, watching TV, and doing yard work. Also, write down how you are feeling—for example, if you are energetic or tired. This will allow you to determine your most productive time of day. After you have recorded your activities for several days, analyze the log to see how you are spending your time. You may be surprised to find how much time you are spending on tasks that you consider to be of low importance. You may also realize that you have the most energy in the morning and choose to schedule more complex tasks at that time.

◆ Is the task worth the time?

Often people spend a great deal of time and energy on tasks that either do not generate many results or are simply a result of self-imposed unrealistic expectations. For example, after keeping an activity log, Tom realized that he spent an entire morning detailing minutes from a meeting the previous day. He also realized that these minutes are hardly read by anyone after the meeting and he had a major deadline the next day. After realizing how much time he spends on meeting details, he spoke with his boss about restructuring the format of the minutes.

Sally, a mother of two young children (one of which has a stomach virus) and a full-time receptionist, stayed up until midnight making cookies for her co-workers. After reviewing her activity log for that day, Sally realized that she spent half the day coordinating an executive meeting and then she cooked dinner for her elderly neighbors before she began baking cookies. Her activity log allowed her to see that she often puts unrealistic expectations on herself to accomplish tasks of low importance. For example, did the co-workers enjoy the cookies enough for her to lose three hours of sleep?

Use your activity log to rate the value of each task: high, medium, or low. Looking back, both Tom and Sally rated the tasks they spent time on as low in value. This process can help you rate activities as they occur so you can manage your time better.

◆ What would you like to spend your time doing?

It is important to consider what you would enjoy spending your time on, since part of effective time management is allowing for recreation and relaxation. Taking time to determine what you enjoy, whether at work or home, can improve your job satisfaction and quality of life. After removing tasks that are low in value from your daily list, use that free time for activities you enjoy doing instead of adding more responsibilities.

◆ What is the best way to spend your time?

Once you have analyzed how you usually spend your time, prioritized your tasks, and determined how you *want* to spend your time, the next step is to plan the best approach to your day. Planning ahead can help you accomplish this. You may have a list of tasks or simply remember what needs to be accomplished. Either way, you will want to plan when you are going to accomplish each task. A good planning method is to use a paper or computerized calendar page that shows each hour of the day and allows you to plan your day in blocks of time. For example, Tom has three major projects

Figure 5-4. Tom's Sample Calendar for Planning Tasks

24th February	
8:00 A.M.	
9:00 A.M.	Work on Penske file
10:00 A.M.	
11:00 A.M.	Janco proposal
12:00 NOON	Lunch
1:00 P.M.	
2:00 P.M.	Task Force meeting
3:00 P.M.	
4:00 P.M.	Work on inventory
5:00 P.M.	
6:00 P.M.	Read after dinner

at work on which he needs to make progress on. His calendar is depicted in Figure 5-4.

On the other hand, Jane, who stays home to watch her three grandchildren and take care of her husband, may have much different plans for her day. Her day's plans are shown in Figure 5-5.

Figure 5-5. Jane's Sample Calendar for Planning Tasks.

24th February	
8:00 A.M.	Make breakfast
9:00 A.M.	Clean stove
10:00 A.M.	Play with children
11:00 A.M.	Nap time/Read book
12:00 NOON	Lunch
1:00 P.M.	Go to bank
2:00 P.M.	Take Jim to doctor
3:00 P.M.	
4:00 P.M.	Take kids to soccer
5:00 P.M.	

Part 5

Relaxation

◆ *What can I gain from relaxation?*

Many people are not aware of the benefits of relaxation and, in fact, many of us do not take the time to relax and unwind from our busy schedules. You have probably heard or said the phrase "I do not have time to relax," when the truth may be that you would feel better if you made time. The following list explains the benefits you may experience by taking the time to relax:

- Decrease in pain
- Decrease in anxiety
- Decrease in depression

TABLE 5-6. Muscle Relaxation

Fists	Clench right fist, then relax. Repeat with left, then both hands.
Biceps	Bend elbows, tense upper arm muscles, relax.
Triceps	Straighten arms and feel tension along back of arms, relax.
Forehead	Wrinkle forehead, frown, relax.
Eyes	Close tightly, relax.
Jaws	Clench jaw, bite teeth together, relax.
Tongue	Press against roof of mouth, relax.
Lips	Press together, relax.
Neck	Press your head straight back, bring head forward to chest, roll to right and left (to the front only), relax.
Shoulders	Shrug one shoulder, then the other, then both, relax.
Chest	Fill lungs with air, hold, exhale.
Stomach	Tighten stomach muscles, relax.
Lower back	Arch up back, make lower back hollow, feel tension along spine, relax.
Buttocks and thighs	Flex by pressing down on heels, straighten knees and flex again, relax.
Calves	Press feet and toes downward and tense calf muscles, relax.
Ankles and Shins	Bend feet toward head feeling tension along shins, relax.

- Decrease in blood pressure
- Decrease in heart rate
- Boosts in the immune system

You probably already know some things that you find relaxing, for example, listening to music, doing puzzles, enjoying nature, seeing a good movie, or exercising. Remember, what relaxes one person may be stressful for another. Keep an open mind when exploring new ideas and use what works best for you.

Several methods are simple enough that they can help you relax on a daily basis. The following list has some tips for successful relaxation:

- Find a quiet place.
- Get in a comfortable position.

- Wear comfortable clothes.
- Clear your mind and focus on the relaxation process.
- Practice routinely (it takes time!).
- Do not expect miracles.

◆ *What are some methods of relaxation that I can use?*

You may want to try progressive muscle relaxation, meditation, deep breathing, or visualization.

Progressive Muscle Relaxation

This method involves tensing a muscle and then relaxing it. As you do this, you will notice the contrast between the feelings of tension in a muscle and relaxation of that muscle (Table 5-6). Try inhaling as you tense a muscle and exhaling as you relax it. Then work at increasing the amount of time you relax and decreasing the amount of time you tense your muscles. If you experience any discomfort or pain with this exercise, please stop and talk to your doctor.

Meditation

Meditation is the practice of focusing your attention on one thing at a time. The intention of meditation is to quiet your thoughts. Some simple ways to help quiet your mind include listening to music, focusing on your breathing, gazing at an object, or repeating a word or phrase. For example, you could repeat the word "one" silently and try to stay focused on this one word. You may prefer to use a line of scripture or a phrase that is meaningful to you. If your attention wanders, gently refocus it on your meditation process.

Deep Breathing

This exercise consists of sitting quietly and comfortably and paying careful attention to your breathing. Sit in a quiet environment, close your eyes, and shift your attention from the outside world and from the responsibilities in your life. Focus on your body and the physical sensations occurring right now. Pay attention to your breathing and follow these steps:

- Inhale very slowly until your lungs are very full.
- Exhale very slowly, blowing all the air out of your lungs.
- Breathe in again very slowly to a count of five.
- Exhale very slowly to a count of five.
- Inhale and exhale at an even pace.
- Continue your slow, deep breathing for approximately 5 to 10 minutes.

Visualization

Visualization (or daydreaming) can be like taking an imaginary vacation. This technique can achieve the same feelings of peacefulness and calmness as meditation, but it is a slightly different technique. Instead of focusing on one single, peaceful thought, visualization helps you to think about a re-

---

Exhibit 5-2. Sample Visualization Exercise

Visualize yourself walking along a mountain path—maybe a favorite place that you have visited before. Feel the cool crispness in the air. Smell the pine needles. See the green of the trees. It's a beautiful day. Feel the sun shining onto your face and arms. You are crossing over a little mountain stream now; stop and feel the coolness of the water on your hands. Notice the mountains around you and in the distance. See the snow at the tops and the timberline below. Breathe in the smells around you. Now you find yourself walking into a valley covered with wildflowers: blues, yellows, pinks, reds—flowers everywhere. You notice a huge bouquet of balloons tied to a tree. You walk toward the balloons. Their colors match the colors of the wild flowers. You reach for the balloons and find that your name is on them. You untie them from the tree and hold them up. As you hold the balloons you realize that they represent all that is bothering or worrying you. Suddenly your arm feels very heavy with the weight of all those balloons. One by one, you let go of the balloons. Each color represents a different worry or stress. Name each balloon with its worry as you let go and feel the relief as the balloon drifts upward. Let go of the last few balloons and watch them all drift up and away. Now, feeling lighter, walk back along the mountain path, over the stream, past the trees. Notice the mountains again in the distance and feel their strength. Slowly, begin to bring yourself back to the room, and when you are ready, open your eyes.

---

laxing environment in full detail. To help you, try reading the text in Exhibit 5-2 quietly to yourself or recording your voice onto a tape so that you can listen to it when you choose. (Your local bookstore may have visualization cassette tapes for you to purchase.)

In summary, balance is important for decreasing stress in your life: balance work with fun, negative with positive, and life's demands with relaxation. The mental balance that you discover just may contribute to a happier, healthier you.

6

Goal Setting

Now that you know which cardiovascular risk factors apply to you and have a good understanding of how to lead a more healthful lifestyle, it is time to create personal goals to help you change the lifestyle habits that have increased your risk in the past. Have you ever said, "I will start that tomorrow"? Setting goals will help get you started.

When you set a goal, keep the word SMART in mind. SMART stands for:

- **S**pecific
- **M**easurable
- **A**ttainable
- **R**ealistic
- **T**imed

◆ *How can I make a specific goal?*

For a goal to be specific, it needs to be clearly understood by everyone who reads your goal, whether they know you or not. An example of a specific goal is to "exercise three days per week for 30 minutes each session." With this type of goal, anyone who reads it will know what you are striving to accomplish. If you just wrote, "exercise more," someone reading it might have any number of ideas about how much you want to work out.

◆ *How can I make a measurable goal?*

You need to be able to measure a goal to see if you attain it. Creating a measurable goal goes hand in hand with creating a specific goal. If you state, "For the next month I will limit meat to four meals per week, and each time the piece of meat will be no larger than the palm of my hand," you will be able to say a definite "yes" or "no" when answering whether or not you attained that goal. On the other hand, if you said you want to "eat less meat for the next month" and were trying to decide whether or not you reached the goal, would you remember how much meat you were eating when you set the goal?

◆ *How can I make an attainable goal?*

For a goal to be attainable, it needs to be something that you can accomplish but also takes some effort. An attainable goal for one person might be to quit smoking "cold turkey," while someone else might need to quit smoking by using nicotine replacement patches and attending a local support group. These goals are both attainable, but each depends on the person who is setting them. The key to setting an attainable goal is to set one that will be somewhat of a challenge for you, but not so difficult that you will get frustrated and quit working on it altogether. In the smoking example, a third goal might be setting a quit date just so that you have something to write down, but knowing that you are not truly ready to quit.

◆ *How can I make a realistic goal?*

For a goal to be realistic, it needs to be realistic to you and your doctor. For example, the goal "to have good blood pressure without taking medication anymore" might sound like a positive goal, but your doctor knows your health history and will be able to tell you how long you will need to take a particular medication. Some medications may be needed for a lifetime. A more realistic goal would be "to monitor my blood pressure weekly and talk with my doctor about how long I will need to be on medication."

◆ *How can I set a timed goal?*

For a goal to be timed it needs to have a beginning and an end. If your goal is to "lose 20 pounds" but you do not give yourself a deadline, it might be easier to put it off. However, if you say, "I want to lose 20 pounds by March 1 of next year," then you have a timed goal to strive for.

Remember that you do not have to set a goal for every risk factor. If there is a risk factor that you know you need to work on but are simply not ready, do not write down a goal. The goal would not be attainable for you right now and might cause unnecessary frustration. Skip it and come back to it later when you have accomplished some of your other goals and are ready to work on the one that is most troublesome.

Take the next several minutes to think about which risk factors you are ready to begin working on. When you have set your goals, it is a good idea to write them down and post them somewhere that you will see often— for example, in your office, on the refrigerator door, or on the bathroom mirror. Remember to talk with your doctor before starting on your goals.

Each time you accomplish a goal, pat yourself on the back and celebrate! Then if you need to, and only when you are ready, write a new one.

A good way to keep track of your goal progress is to keep a journal of your accomplishments. That way, as you work towards difficult goals that may seem nearly impossible to reach, you can refer back to the journal and view your successes. By keeping track of where you started, you can see small accomplishments as well as large ones.

Glossary

Abnormal Heart Rhythm: Any heart rhythm that is not a normal sinus rhythm, which is defined as a heart rate of 60 to 100 beats per minute.

Adrenaline: A hormone occurring naturally in the body and also man made (called epinephrine) for medical use.

Amino acid: An organic compound that is considered a "building block" of protein molecules.

Angina: Chest discomfort caused by lack of oxygen to the heart, which may include a feeling of choking, suffocation or crushing pressure, and pain.

Angiogram: An x-ray picture of the heart and vessels of the heart. X-ray films are taken while a substance that will show up on x-ray films is injected into a vein or directly into the heart.

Angioplasty: A surgical procedure in which a catheter is inserted, usually at the groin, and fed up to the coronary arteries. When a blockage in the coronary arteries is reached, a balloon on the end of the catheter is inflated to push the blockage to the walls of the artery. This procedure increases the lumen of the artery.

Artery: A blood vessel that carries oxygenated blood away from the heart to the body.

Atherosclerosis: A term used to describe diseases in which the walls of the artery become thickened and lose the ability to stretch. This thickening is due to cholesterol, lipids, and other cellular waste matter (including calcium) being deposited in the inner layers of the artery.

Atrial fibrillation: An electrical abnormality of the heart muscle where the atria contract in an irregular rhythm, which may be fast. Symptoms may include a feeling of palpitations or "fluttering" in the chest or chest discomfort, weakness, faintness, breathlessness, or nothing at all.

Atrial flutter: An electrical abnormality of the heart muscle in which the atria (the top chambers of the heart) contract rapidly at approximately 300 beats per minute. The ventricles (the bottom chambers of the heart) usually contract at about 150 beats per minute. This is a regular, although fast, rhythm.

Blood clot: A semi-solid mass that is the end result of the clotting process in blood.

Blood pressure: A measure of the force of blood against the arterial walls. Blood pressure is measured in millimeters of mercury.

Blood vessel: Any one of the network of tubes that carries blood.

Body Mass Index (BMI): Mathematically this is weight in kilometers divided by height in meters squared. BMI is a measure of obesity.

Bradycardia: An electrical abnormality of the heart muscle. The heart contracts normally, but at a slow rate of less than 60 beats per minute.

Carbon monoxide: An odorless, colorless gas which is poisonous. The burning of fuel in an area of poor oxygen supply produces carbon monoxide.

Cardiologist: A medical doctor who specializes in diseases of the heart.

Cardiomyopathy: A disease of the myocardium, which is the middle layer of the walls of the heart.

Cardiovascular disease: The description used for several abnormal conditions that are characterized by improper function of the heart and blood vessels.

Cerebrovascular accident: A general term which is used to describe the lack of oxygen to the brain or bleeding lesions within the blood vessels of the brain. This cerebrovascular accident is commonly referred to as a "stroke."

Cholesterol: A substance that is closely related to fat and is found in animal tissues, egg yolks, various oils, fats, the nerve tissue of the brain and spinal cord, the liver, the kidneys, and the adrenal glands.

Cholesterol free: A descriptive term used on a food label that means the product has less than two milligrams of cholesterol per serving and less than or equal to two grams of saturated fat per serving.

Claudication: A weakness of the legs and cramp-like pains in the calves, thighs, and/or buttocks. It is caused by poor circulation of blood to the leg muscles and is often accompanied by atherosclerosis.

Congestive heart failure: A temporary or ongoing condition that is a result of the heart not being able to provide satisfactory blood circulation.

Coronary artery: One of the main arteries that lie on the heart and are responsible for supplying the heart with blood. The coronary arteries include the left main, the left anterior descending artery, the right coronary artery, and the circumflex artery.

Coronary artery disease: A narrowing of the coronary arteries that is severe enough to prevent the necessary amount of blood from getting to the myocardium (the middle layer of the walls of the heart).

Cortisol: A chemical substance that is produced in the body and is also man made for medical use to help with inflammation.

Diabetes mellitus: A disease that is characterized by excessive urination. Diabetes mellitus has two categories: insulin-dependent (Type I) and non–insulin-dependent (Type II). Type II diabetes occurs more often than Type I and is most common in individuals over 40 years of age.

Echocardiogram: A procedure used to study the structure and motion of the heart by using ultrasonic waves (sound waves).

Endorphin: A molecule produced by the body that has pain-suppressing actions. It is believed that endorphins are released when pain impulses are triggered, providing natural pain control. The euphoric feeling, sometimes termed the "runner's high" that people have after exercise, is thought to be from the production of endorphins.

Electrocardiogram (EKG, ECG): A paper record of the electrical impulses of the heart muscle.

Enzyme: A protein produced by living cells that modifies the rate of chemical reactions in the body.

Exercise electrocardiogram: A stress test involving exercise that is used to determine the diagnosis of coronary artery disease. An exercise electrocardiogram is recorded as a person walks on a treadmill, pedals a bicycle, or completes some other exercise task.

Exercise stress test: See Exercise electrocardiogram.

Fat free: A descriptive term used on a food label that means the product has less than 0.5 grams of fat per serving.

Fluid retention: The body's inability to get rid of excess fluid.

Glucose: A sugar found in certain foods such as fruit. It is also an important source of energy for humans and animals.

Heart attack: See Myocardial infarction.

Heart rate, resting: The number of times the heart contracts (beats) in one minute. A normal resting heart rate is anywhere from 60 to 100 beats per minute.

Heart rate, target: The estimated number of times the heart should contract (beat) while exercising. The target heart rate can be estimated by a mathematical equation or from the results of an exercise stress test, which is performed by a medical doctor.

Heart valve disorder: The four valves in the heart open and close to keep blood flowing in the proper direction. Heart valve disorder is a common term to describe a condition where any one of the valves does not work properly, causing blood flow to change direction or slow down.

High Density Lipoprotein (HDL): A lipoprotein is made up of cholesterol, phospholipid, and triglyceride. A high-density lipoprotein (HDL) is a lipoprotein that contains a high level of protein. HDL is sometimes referred to as "healthy" or "good," and a high level of HDL is desirable.

Homocysteine: An amino-acid (protein). There is evidence that a high level of homocysteine in the blood is associated with an increased risk of developing coronary artery disease.

Internal medicine: A branch of medicine that is specifically focused on the study of the internal organs and the diagnosis and treatment of diseases affecting the organs.

Lipid levels: The term lipid level refers to the amount of lipids (fat) found in the bloodstream.

Low calorie: A descriptive term used on a food label that means the product has no more than 40 calories per serving.

Low-Density Lipoprotein (LDL): A lipoprotein is made up of cholesterol, phospholipid, and triglyceride. A low-density lipoprotein (LDL) is a lipoprotein that contains a low level of protein. LDL is sometimes referred to as "lousy" or "bad," and a low level of LDL is desirable.

Low sodium: A descriptive term used on a food label that means the product has no more than 140 milligrams of sodium per serving.

Lumen: The channel of the inside of a blood vessel.

Meditation: To reflect on, to ponder; to engage in contemplation.

Monitor: A device used to document or control an activity or process.

Myocardial infarction (heart attack): A complete blockage of a coronary artery caused by atherosclerosis or a blood clot. When a complete blockage occurs, the heart muscle cannot get the oxygen it needs to function and becomes permanently damaged.

Nicotine replacement therapy: Any number of therapies that send nicotine into the body to be used in place of cigarettes, cigars, chew, or dip. The therapy may be in the form of patches, gum, or cigarette-like tubes. Nicotine replacement therapy is gradually decreased and then stopped to help a person quit using tobacco.

Osteoporosis: A disorder in which the bones become abnormally thin. It occurs most frequently in women who are post menopausal.

Peripheral vascular disease: Any condition that is abnormal and that affects the blood vessels outside the heart and lymphatic vessels.

Plaque: A patch of atherosclerosis.

Platelet: The smallest of the cells in the blood. Platelets are necessary for blood clotting, for example, to stop a cut from bleeding.

Premature Atrial Contraction (PAC): An abnormal heart rhythm where the atrium (one of the two top chambers of the heart) contracts before the normal contraction cycle.

Premature Ventricular Contraction (PVC): An abnormal heart rhythm where the ventricle (one of the two bottom chambers of the heart) contracts before the normal contraction cycle.

Progressive muscle relaxation: A method of relaxation where a person progressively tightens or tenses each muscle or muscle group and then relaxes it. Usually the exercise starts at the head and ends at the feet.

Resting heart rate: See Heart rate, resting.

Risk Factor: A chemical, psychological, physiological, or genetic element (or an element in the environment) that is thought to increase the probability of an individual developing a disease.

Sinoatrial node (SA node): A grouping of hundreds of cells located in the right upper chamber (atrium) of the heart. The SA node is responsible for starting the electrical impulse that travels throughout the heart, causing it to contract (beat).

Stent: A wire-mesh device that is placed into an artery to increase the blood flow through the artery.

Stress: The physical or psychological factors that individuals experience. The factors may be positive or negative. Examples include injury, fear, joy, and anxiety.

Stressor: Anything that causes physical or mental wear and tear on the body.

Stroke: See Cerebrovascular Accident.

Tachycardia: An electrical abnormality of the heart muscle. The heart contracts normally, but at a rate of more than 100 beats per minute.

Triglyceride: A lipid (fat) that is used by the body for energy.

Valve: A natural or artificial structure that prevents fluid from traveling in the wrong direction.

Vein: One of the many blood vessels that carries non-oxygenated blood from the body back to the heart.

Visualization: The act of forming a mental image or vision.

References and Resources

REFERENCES

American Diabetes Association. (1999). Clinical practice recommendations. *Diabetes Care, 22* (Suppl.), S1–114.

Berkman, L. F., Leo-Summer, L. and Horwitz, R.I. (1992). Emotional support and survival after myocardial infarction. *Annals of Internal Medicine,* 117, 1003–1009.

Berkow, R., Fletcher, A. J. & Beers, M. H. (Eds.). (1992). *The Merck Manual of Diagnosis and Therapy,* 16th Edition. Rahway, N.J.: Merck Research Laboratories.

Berube, M. S., Neely, D. J. & DeVinne, P. B. (Eds.). (1985). *American Heritage Dictionary,* 2nd college edition. Boston, Mass.: Houghton Mifflin Co.

Blumenthal, J. A., O'Connor, C., Hinderliter, A., Fath, K., Hegde, S. B., Miller, G., Puma, J., Sessions, W., Sheps, D., Zakhary, B. & Williams, R. B. (1997). Psychosocial factors and coronary disease. A national multicenter clinical trial (ENRICHD) with a North Carolina focus. *North Carolina Medical Journal.* 58(6): 440–444.

Borg, G. (1998). *Borg's Perceived Exertion and Pain Scales.* Champaign, Ill.: Human Kinetics.

Dawber, T. R. (1980). *The Framingham Study.* Cambridge, Mass.: Harvard University Press.

Eliot, R. S. & Breo, D. L. (1989). *Is It Worth Dying For?* New York, N.Y.: Bantam Books.

Ellis, A. & Lange, A. (1994). *How to keep people from pushing your buttons.* New York, N.Y.: Birch Lane Publishers.

Everson, S. A., Kauhanen, J., Kaplan, G. A., Goldberg, D. E., Julkunen, J, Tuomilehto, J. & Salonen, J. T. (1997). Hostility and increased risk of mortality and acute myocardial infarction: the mediating role of behavioral risk factors. *American Journal of Epidemiology,* 146(2):142–152.

Franklin, B. A., Whaley, M. H., & Howley, E. T. (Eds.) (2000). *American College of Sports Medicine Guidelines for Exercise Testing and Prescription,* 6th edition. Baltimore, Md.: Lippincott Williams & Wilkins.

Frasure-Smith, N., Lesperance, F. & Talajic, M. (1993). Depression following myocardial infarction. Impact on 6-month survival. *JAMA,* 270(15): 1819–1825.

Glanze, W. D., Anderson, K. N. & Anderson, L. E. (Eds.). (1990). *Mosby's Medical Dictionary,* revised 3rd edition. St. Louis, Mo.: The C.V. Mosby Co.

Guyton, A. (1981). *Textbook of Medical Physiology,* 9th Edition. Philadelphia, Pa., W. B. Saunders Company.

Jolley, W. (1999). *A Setback is a Setup for a Comeback.* New York, N.Y.: St. Martin's Press.

King, K. B. (1997). Psychologic and social aspects of cardiovascular disease. *Annals of Behavioral Medicine.* 19(3):264–270.

Miller, M. A. & Rahe, R. H. (1997). Life changes scaling for the 1990's, *Journal of Psychosomatic Research,* 43(3):279–292.

Taylor, E. J. (Ed.). (1988). *Dorland's Illustrated Medical Dictionary,* 27th Edition. Philadelphia, Pa.: W. B. Saunders Company.

Thomas, C. L. (Ed.). (1993). *Taber's Cyclopedic Medical Dictionary,* 18th Edition. Philadelphia, Pa.: F. A. Davis Company.

United States Department of Agriculture, Center for Nutrition Policy and Promotion. (1996). The Food Guide Pyramid, *Home and Garden Bulletin Number 252.*

Wetmore, D. E. (2000). *Time management and personal productivity seminars.* [On-line]. Available: www.balancetime.com.

Williams, R. and Williams, V. (1993). *Anger Kills.* New York, N.Y.: Times Books.

RESOURCES

American Cancer Society
American College of Cardiology
American Diabetes Association
American Dietetic Association
American Heart Association
American Journal of Cardiology
Centers for Disease Control and Prevention
Hospital Educators Resource Catalogue, Inc
Mindtools.com
National Heart, Lung and Blood Institute
National Lipid Education Council
National Weather Service Office (Newport, North Carolina)
United States Department of Health and Human Services